Nik Zan<

CHILDREN
OF THE TIDE

弄潮兒

AN EXPLORATION OF SURFING
IN DYNASTIC CHINA

ON THE COVER
Detail from the 500 Luohans
of the Bamboo Temple, Kunming.
Bas-relief by Li Guangxiu, 1880.

EDITING
Sam Bleakley
sambleakley.co.uk

GRAPHIC DESIGN
studiovisuale.it

PRINTED IN ITALY BY
Grafiche Antiga

PLEASE VISIT
[O] @childrenofthetide_thebook
[f] @childrenofthetide

Distributed in the UK
and Europe by Cordee Ltd
First edition 2019.

For my beautiful mum Silvana
Thank you for letting this monkey roam free

CONTENTS

'The Great Sage was gazing at the Eastern Ocean,
sighing sadly at being driven away by the Tang Priest.
'I haven't been this way for five hundred years,'
he said. As he looked at the sea,

Vast were the misty waters,
Boundless the mighty waves.
The vast and misty waters stretched to the Milky Way;
The boundless and mighty waves were linked
to the earth's arteries.
The tides came surging,
The waters swirled around.
The surging tides
Roared like the thunder in spring;
The swirling waters
Howled like a summer hurricane.
The blessed ancients riding on dragons
Surely must have frowned as they came and went;
Immortal youths flying on cranes
Certainly felt anxious as they passed above.'

- SU WUKONG (THE MONKEY KING)
IN **JOURNEY TO THE WEST** BY WU CHENG'EN

CHAPTER ONE

THE TEMPLE OF SURFING BUDDHAS

A Chinese proverb says that a ten-thousand-miles journey starts with a single step. My first step into China as a kid at home in Ferrara, Italy, was reading *Journey to the West*, an epic of Ming dynasty folklore filled with adventure, comedy and mysticism. I would spend hours following Sun Wukong, the Monkey King, who, according to author Wu Cheng'en, was so clever he could 'conceive emptiness' through Daoist and Buddhist meditation. The Monkey was irreverent and witty, but he had acquired such special magical powers that the Buddha himself recruited him to escort the monk Xuanzang to India and back to retrieve Buddhist sutras. But the heart of the Monkey King's appeal is his human fallibility- he is greedy, selfish and prone to sudden mood swings. He defies divine authority, laughs at attempts to be controlled, and leaves chaos in his wake. But you know that there is fundamental good within him.

I was born in 1968, year of the monkey. As a rebellious kid, a surfer, skater and punk-rocker, I could see myself in the Monkey King's misbehaviour. He is the bad and bored boy who needs a sense of purpose to come good. His sense of purpose was the quest to retrieve the Buddhist sutras. My sense of purpose was surfing. Like the Monkey King, I craved for something intense and fulfilling. I wanted a travelling life, away from the norm, packed with adventure and exposure to cultures other than my own. As crazy as it sounds, studying Chinese in Venice in the late 1980s seemed to promise an exciting future, exploring waves and cultures in my journey to the east.

Armed with the ability to speak Mandarin, I rode a lot of good waves along the coastline of China across various trips in the 1990s and 2000s in what *Journey to the West* called the 'Southern Ocean'. Then, in 2006, I surfed my way through Hainan island and Hong Kong before heading inland. I fantasised about witnessing first-hand the lofty peaks, misty valleys, bamboo grooves and monasteries so brilliantly described in *Journey to the West*. Yunnan Province seemed to fit the bill.

In the West we tend to demonise China's recent Communist history (largely from gross misunderstanding), but China is the oldest civilisation on earth, continuous for 25 centuries, where Daoism, Confucianism and Buddhism have played a powerful role as the perfect triangle of human qualities - Daoism's connection with nature; Confucianism's code of manners; and Buddhism's rejection of self-interest. Yunnan is a true celebration of the cultural lure of China. It is a multi-ethnic area just north of the Tropics bordering Vietnam, Laos and Thailand. It has been a Buddhist stronghold and a place where Daoism and the shamanic practices of ethnic groups such as the Naxi have mixed freely, and the sound of the wind through a bamboo grove is a gesture of enlightenment. It has also been a trade centre on the southwestern route of the Silk Road for two millennia, linking the fertile provinces of the east with the Tibetan Plateau and the Brahmaputra and Ganges delta. Here, geography has shaped a unique imagination of the world.

Kunming is the humid capital of Yunnan, now over-populated with six million people, rising awkwardly at an altitude of 1,900 metres, but trapped on three sides by steep karst mountains and flanked to the south by the willow beds of lake Dian. Humans have so often turned their back on the heritage of sustainability that Daoism venerates, and sadly this 40 km long reservoir is now so polluted from population pressures and economic growth

that its waters are unsuitable even for irrigation. Despite the fact
that this was a place where monks would return to the rhythms
and presence of nature, typified by the mountain man in solitary
retreat, rapid industrialisation has left many scars on the environment. But in spite of its scale and industrial output, Kunming
does still retain the flavour of an agricultural and traditional
China where the wind still smells pure. Naxi farmers, and other ethnic groups - such as the Zhuang and Miao - travel down
from the hills in pride, with their best products in huge pat-
terned wicker baskets to sell in the markets inside the city walls
maintaining an unbroken tradition. These riches include vegetables and flowers from the valleys, tropical fruits from the lowlands, fragrant mushrooms and small sweet chestnuts from the
mountain slopes. Most famous of all is *pu'er* (black) tea that has
grown wild in the surrounding forests for thousands of years,
and is now tendered to perfection in tea terraces. It is stored in
round bricks, the longer the better, with a 20-years-old harvest
costing fortunes.

Within minutes of leaving Kunming city, the grey hues are replaced by a patchwork of tea plantations, rice fields, then towering bamboo groves, papaya trees and pine forests. Big and bushy
hemp also grows wild here. Many locals chew on its seeds, loom
its fibre for cloth and sell thick sticky buds to a few intrepid backpackers and adventure tourists learning about the essence of
Daoism and stoned stiff.

Most of them, including myself, were likely inspired to follow
in the footsteps of the late, great Bruce Chatwin whose article 'In
China: Rock's Kingdom' published in the *New York Times* in 1986
popularised Yunnan in the western imagination. Chatwin was
becoming fascinated by Daoist culture, and suffering from (un-
beknown to him at the time) early symptoms of HIV. He went to
Baisha village just outside Lijiang to consult Yunnanese herbalist

He Shixiu, or Dr Ho as Chatwin called him, celebrating 'the Tao-ist (another way of spelling 'Daoist') physician in the Jade Drag-on Mountains'. During the Cultural Revolution that temporarily suppressed the traditional culture of China, Chairman Mao's Red Guards had forbidden Dr Ho to practice medicine. He was either in prison, or hiding in the mountains, where he discovered many rare herbs. But the new 'open door' policy after Mao's death in the late 1970s had allowed Dr Ho to practice again. Chatwin's travel guide Joseph Rock (hence the article's name 'Rock's King-dom') - an eccentric Austro-American botanist and explorer who for many years lived in Lijiang - inspired Dr Ho and taught him English. Chatwin died in 1989 at the age of 48. Perhaps there might there have been an *In Yunnan* book had he lived longer. If that was the case, there would certainly be a lot more stoned backpackers here.

While Kunming has skyrocketed in size, looking towards the mountains from the city, not much has changed since the Mon-key King traversed this landscape and its ubiquitous sub-tropical mist on his westbound journey. The Buddhist temples nestled in the mountains have survived the purges of the Cultural Revolu-tion and remain surrounded by lush steaming foliage refusing the re-writing of history.

I was heading for one of these very temples located on Mount Yuan 10 km northwest of Kunming. The Qiongzhu Temple (筇竹寺 or Bamboo Temple in reference to the surrounding *qiongzhuea* bamboo) was established during the Yuan dynasty (1271-1368) and the first centre of Chan Buddhism that caravans would encoun-ter entering from India. Chan Buddhism evolved between the 5th and 6th centuries from the interaction between Indian Mahāyāna Buddhism and Chinese Daoism. Under the 唐 Táng (618-907) and 宋 Sòng dynasties (960-1279) Chan Buddhism reached a 'golden age' and took its definitive shape, involving yogic breathing practices, and use of *koans* (riddles and conundrums) for study, meditation and enlightenment, migrated to Japan, and further refined to become Zen Buddhism.

In the 1880s a fire sadly devastated parts of the Bamboo Temple, but the reigning Emperor Guangxu (1871-1908) of the 清 Qīng dynasty (1644-1912) ordered a rebuild. The renovation included 500 life-size statues of Buddhist deities commissioned to a well-known artist named Li Guangxiu. None of the individually carved clay figures are identical. Daoist masters, Muslim merchants from the northwestern region of Xinjiang, Hindu Brahmins with brown curly hair, and, oddly enough, Jesus himself can be spotted among the statues. Sanctity, as proclaimed by Chan Buddhism, is not the monopoly of any religion, but a sudden state of mind attainable by anyone.

600 km from the closest beach, the salt-stain of my last surf long since washed off, you can imagine my surprise when I walked into the so called Precious Hall of The Great Hero to see 30 figures riding a green-blue wave, performing manoeuvres and standing on top of mythological animals. A few steps further into the corridor and my gaze fell on the eyes of the central figure of the installation: a surfer, in a perfect sideways stance, riding a left-hander with a stoked grin on his face. My jaw dropped. I came out in a cold sweat.

Most of the statues share his same ecstatic expression, their eyes fixed a few metres in front of their watercraft as if anticipating a promising wave section to shape up ahead. 'Only a surfer knows the feeling'. A line suddenly linked two cultures that had ruled my life: surfing and China. This crowded wave was a turning point, one that would not rely on maps and weather forecasts for exploration, but on reading and translating ancient Chinese documents. My two loves had converged.

As I regained composure I lit a full box of ritual incense sticks for the main Bodhisattva of the Temple. Then I went looking for the Abbot in search of information.

I found him in his studio. He was a corpulent Han Chinese in his early 50s, clad in the grey-blue robes worn during 'unofficial' workdays and drinking out of a rusty metal mug. The earthy smell of *pu'er* tea filled the room. It was so strong I could almost taste the fermented, bitter flavour. Behind his desk there was a two-metres-tall scroll containing one elongated character 禪 *chán* meaning 'meditation'. A pile of books, sporting bright cartoonish Bodhisattvas, towered next to a mess of printed Xcel sheets and bowl of chewed up sunflower seeds.

I introduced myself in my best Mandarin as 'a practicing Buddhist from Europe' (not actually true, but sure to capture his attention) visiting notable temples on my way from Hainan to Tibet in my search to learn more about Buddhist art. I had the perfect artefact for the story. The Abbot eyed my sandalwood 18 beads rosary typical of the Mahayana school, stood up, smiled and shook my hand with approval.

"How can I help you, foreign believer?" he said in Mandarin. "Surfing, Master," I answered, fully knowing we'd only be speaking in Mandarin. "I'd like to know about those statues I have seen in the prayer hall." The Abbot was dumbstruck. He clearly couldn't understand the word *chōng làng* (冲浪 modern Chinese for 'surfing' used since the 1970s).

After a few attempts to define 'surfing', the word continued to ring no bells for him. So I asked if he'd walk with me to the prayer hall. He followed, and we stopped in front of the wave. I pointed at the 'surfers' and repeated the question. "Master, who are these men and what are they doing? Are they real people or imaginary characters?" "Those are *luohan*, living saints, real people like me and you, who have followed the scriptures and attained enlightenment."

In the Buddhist pantheon, *luohan* ('*arhat*' in Sanskrit) is the first stage of sanctity, the only one attainable by a physical person. *Luohan* status is just under Bodhisattva, who by definition can only be a divine entity. The Abbot's explanation continued, packed with religious detail, "They represent Shakyamuni's (Buddhism originates in the teachings of Shakyamuni - or Gautama Siddhartha - who was born in what is now Nepal some 2,500 years ago) best disciples, entrusted by him to remain in the world and not to enter Nirvana until Maitreya, the oncoming Buddha, appears and brings in a new era." "But why are they on a wave? Why are they...surfing?" The Abbot raised his eyebrows with confusion. "What is this activity you talk about?" "Surfing is just this," I said, pointing at a regular-footed *luohan* riding a wave. "The art of riding waves on a board, and achieving unity with nature." "Oh, I know what *chong lang* is. I've seen it on television. But we don't call this surfing."

I was confused. Chan Buddhism is famous for its 公案 *gōngàn* (*kōan* in Japanese) - paradoxical riddles, tales bound to demolish the dry rational gears of logical thought, and substitute them with meditation and sudden enlightenment. "They ride waves, but they are not surfing?" I asked. "They are enjoying life at its utmost. They are *nong chao er*."

I rushed to my moleskin and asked the Abbot to scribble down those three characters. He wrote '弄潮兒 *nòng cháo ér*' in a very quick 'grass style', the fastest form of cursive.

A large group of Chinese tourists entered the courtyard, the Abbot passed me back the moleskin, joined his hands in a *mudra* pose to signal his departure, then reached for his Nokia now vibrating in his shirt pocket. I lowered my head respectfully, but insisted, "Where can I find information on these people? Are they still doing it?" "You should look for them in Hangzhou," he said, gesturing he needed to answer his mobile. I bowed. He left.

This book is my journey recovering the *nong chao er* in the Bamboo Temple of Surfing Buddhas, from a freshman in Venice studying Chinese, to exploring the coastline of China for empty waves, to the untold history of wave-riding in dynastic China that goes back to the 9th century. It tells of my love affair with two of the most refined and complicated cultures I have had the luck to encounter: wave-riding and China, both blessed with paradox. No two cultural environments seem to be further apart. How does the profundity of Daoism, or the pragmatic value complex of Confucianism, relate to an activity that has produced *kowabunga* handshakes and the stereotypical stoned Californian surfer dude (Jeff Spiccoli, played by Sean Penn in Amy Heckerling's film *Fast Times at Ridgemont High* 1982)? At a first glance they don't, but Spiccoli would have loved the Yunnan weed, and if you take the time to search in the *mare magnum* of dynastic history with the passion of a surf explorer, you'll find out that China and wave-riding do cross paths, at many levels, starting from 1,200 years ago.

CHAPTER ONE — THE TEMPLE OF SURFING BUDDHAS

CHAPTER TWO

DAY ONE ON THE SILK ROAD

My Silk Road started in Ferrara, Italy, where I grew up developing a strange fascination with China and Chinese folklore, fuelled by reading *Journey to the West* and Laozi's *Dao De Jing* (*The Classic of the Way and Its Virtue*). And a degree in Sinology from the Department of Oriental Studies in Venice seemed to promise a closer connection to China's rich history, a life away from the norm, a route east into the future of an ancient culture, out of the cosy provincial boredom I was born into.

I went to one of the most rigid high schools in Italy. Ferrara's infamous Liceo Roiti was a hotbed of reactionary teachers, where the local *intelligentsia* sent their spoilt kids to be educated 'the old way', ripe with memorisation and humiliation. The only lesson that fired me up was Philosophy and the day we had a reserve teacher who had some interest in Asian folklore. She had travelled extensively and told us the legend of Pangu, the mythical creator of China, born from the egg of chaos and grown to fill the space between *Di* (the earth) and *Tian* (the heavens). For 18 thousand years Pan Ku chiseled the earth into its present form with the aid of a dragon, a unicorn, a phoenix, and a tortoise. When he died, his eyes became the sun and moon, while his body turned into the soil, rivers, rain, and ocean. His sundry parasites, meanwhile, transformed into humans.

But letting your imagination roam free was not the norm at Liceo Roiti. Math, Latin, Chemistry and Physics filled the weeks.

I had come to hate them all. My marks never went above sixty per cent. The teachers kept telling my parents that I was smart, spoke great English, but was insubordinate. "He needs discipline," they concluded. I ignored them. I disrespected the teachers and hated their archaic methods. I also felt different from my classmates. They were typical children of the early 1980s: Timberland shoes, Moncler jackets and Duran Duran blasting out of their Sony Walkman. I had been to California, Australia, the UK and dreamed of travelling to China. I could read Bruce Chatwin, Jack Kerouac and Wu Cheng'en in English. I had dreadlocks, listened to Minor Threat and Black Flag. And I didn't mind missing class to chase surf.

My friends aimed to become Engineers, Doctors, Lawyers. Not for me. My room was filled with poetry books, maps, punk concert posters, skateboards and seafaring gear. I had made my own poster written in English from Laozi's *Dao De Jing* repeating lines about the *yin* and *yang*: *As soon as beauty is known by the world as beautiful, it becomes ugly. As soon as virtue is being known as something good, it becomes evil. Therefore being and non-being give birth to each other. Difficult and easy accomplish each other. Long and short form each other. High and low distinguish each other. Sound and tone harmonise each other. Before and after follow each other as a sequence. Realising this, the saint performs effortlessly according to the natural Way without personal desire, and practices the wordless teaching through one's deeds.* I didn't really know what it all meant, but next to the poster I had the things I valued: spear guns, wetsuits, knives, fins and fishing rods. And above all, my surfboard hung from the ceiling, and I was restless to surf my local spot in Ravenna every time a swell hit.

Ravenna, populated by 150,000, has faded from past glories. It has been a capital three times: Western Roman Empire (402-476), Ostrogoth Kingdom (493-553) and Byzantium (568-751). The

mosaics inside San Vitale's cathedral tell stories of sea faring 21
Byzantine people sailing in and out a walled city harbour. By the
time I was growing up, Ravenna had already turned away from
the coast, no longer salt-stained, but surviving on agriculture.
The old city harbour, and all the canals, now lay buried in sand,
swallowed by the ever-changing coastlines south of the huge Po
Delta. Instead, post war development led by the *Democrazia Cris-
tinana* (Christian Democracy, who dominated Italian politics for
fifty years) created a vast petrochemical industry and a deep-water port in Marina Di Ravenna, 10 km to the east.

If you have visited other towns lining the Adriatic coast, like
Trieste, Ancona, Vasto, or Otranto on the heel of Italy's boot, you
may have noticed what poet Eugenio Montale described as an
'eastern anxiety' in *The Occasions*. It's a slow burning awareness
that all the best times have already happened, and most things
worth living for are taking place elsewhere, upwind, east.

Perhaps this feeling is caused by the peculiar weather pattern
these towns are exposed to. The Mediterranean here is not deep
enough to mitigate continental weather. Air temperatures vary
from a sub polar -10°C in the dead of winter, to tropical 40°C in
midsummer. Water temperatures also rise and fall radically. The
main force behind such drastic changes is the northeast wind
known as Bora. The peculiar fishy smell of Bora meant 'waves'
to a whole generation of Adriatic-based surfers, born long before
internet weather forecasts, when sensorial stimuli, not satellite
models, mattered.

A summertime Bora is very different to a wintertime Bora,
when continental high pressure extends from Croatia (in former Yugoslavia), all the way to the East Japan Sea, and everyone's
teeth - from Venice to Vladivostok (7,000 km east on the same latitude) - are chattering to below zero temperatures. As an Adriatic

surfer I cherished Bora's moods and short-fetch waves. I loved the quick change of light triggered by a drop in humidity. But most of all I was intrigued by the smell. I hadn't been east yet, but it reminded me of the vicinity of the caravan routes along the ancient silk road, and of the lure of a long trip up wind. It was scary but electrifying. It smelled alive. And the sea's skin was an animal waking, stretching and unfurling, a playground to surf.

Present for over 100 days per year, Bora is the undisputed *primo violino* of the Eastern Mediterranean weather symphony. Surfers and mariners know that it can arise abruptly, with minimal signs, and reach 60 to 80 knots in a matter of hours. The waves it generates are clustered, short in period but can become dangerously big in size. Underestimate Bora's early signs and it can crush your boat, drown you, or rejuvenate your soul with an unforgettable surf session. Bora's tempo is also peculiar. It always blows for an odd number of days, creating a ternary beat that seems to make the air dance as if in a waltz, with high pitch wind solos and syncopated interludes of crystal clear stillness. Once the stage is set, Bora can keep dancing for three, five, sometimes up to nine days.

In spite of its soft sounding name, shared by languages from Slovenia (*Burja*) to Poland (*Burza*) and Turkey, Bora is a powerhouse. The name comes from the demigod Boreas son of Eos (goddess of dawn) and of the titan Astraeus. Greek mythology depicts Boreas as an old, grumpy man with ruffled hair and a grey beard. His bad temper is renowned. It was a nine day long blow from Boreas that cursed Odysseus' return from the war in Troy, throwing him and his crew from Cape Meleas (the southernmost tip of the Peloponnesian peninsula) into a monster-ridden land of myth. It took Odysseus ten years to recover from that one Bora storm to create the archetypal 'journey' and homecoming story that has rinsed the Western psyche with wanderlust.

Homer may have been blind, but he depicted these swells brilliantly in the repeating motif of 'the wine-dark sea'. 'Land and sky were hidden in thick clouds, and night sprang forth out of the heavens,' Homer wrote in *The Odyssey*. Further, 'Jove concealed evil against him, and made it blow hard, 'till waves ran mountains high.' Every port in the eastern Mediterranean, from Ravenna to Heraklion in Crete, has been designed to offer shelter from this meteorological beast.

Not surprisingly, Adriatic surfers were more akin to ancient seafaring crew members than modern day wave riding hipsters. In between swells we hung out around the docks and smoky bars of Marina di Ravenna, checking tide charts, waiting for the onshore gale to die out, or listening to a fisherman's latest report. These fishermen were mainly *cozzari*, local families owning a *bragozzo*, a crude 15 metres long boat. They farmed *cozze* (mussels) a few kilometres offshore. Their nearshore job says a lot about Ravenna's refusal to take to the waters full on. *Cozzari* lacked the perseverance of farmers and the courage of deep-sea fishermen, but, as surfers, we shared the same playground.

When Bora blew, the flat and wide *bragozzo* boats simply could not operate in rough conditions. The art of the *cozzari* was anticipating Bora and working the mussel beds before it arrived. Then they usually waited one or three or seven days before going back out and checking the damage to the mussels.

Several *cozzari* had picked up surfing. Our main spot was the south side of the 2.8 km long harbour wall, where a set of sandbanks combed the short-fetched northeast surf into brown coloured left handers. Because of the shallow bathymetry, waves at this spot were not measured in meters, but using five fishing houses on stilts called *capanno*, built right on the wall. The first *capanno* was 500 meters from the shore. Waves breaking there meant belly to shoulder high. The second and third had the best banks, and were able to throw some great shape with a southeast Sirocco swell. The fourth and fifth *capanno* broke only a few times a year when it was over two metres. On a good day you could take off two kilometres out at sea and ride all the way to shore.

Our weather forecasting tool was the 48 hours marine report, produced twice a day by the *Aeronautica Militare* (Italian Air Force), and distributed via radio, toll phone or fax. Wave size was not mentioned, so we had to work that out using wind force, direction and local knowledge. The margin for error was huge. Forecasting surf in Ravenna was as much art as science. Southerly swells named Sirocco (from Arabic *shurhùq* meaning southern wind) were totally unpredictable. Unexpected low pressures located over 1,000 km away generate them. They would climb up the Adriatic and hit us with long period (hence high quality) conditions. Sirocco was Bora's nemesis. Waves would come out of nowhere accompanied by no smell or particular cloud formation. You needed to live on the beach to tap into such unexpected perfection. It could just last a few hours, and then disappear. In contrast, Bora was somehow more democratic, lower in quality, but user friendly. Even without forecasts, a trained nose could literally smell Bora coming 24 hours in advance.

Surfing started in Ravenna in the late 1970s. Exposed to both southeast and northeast swell, waves are surprisingly frequent, around 120 days a year. Yet because of the limited scale of the sea, the period is doomed to stay in the 3 to 8 seconds range. Good waves may only last one or two hours. Right time and right place are mandatory. 'You just missed it' was the most injurious of insults.

Surfers from the first generation had dubious part-time jobs (or family money) that left them plenty of free time. Lodovico

'Guancia' Baroncelli was the pioneer. He had single-handedly 'invented' surfing in the Adriatic, bringing back the first surfboards from trips to California. He also had a license for Cessna aircrafts and had mapped 30 km of coast around Ravenna. He had a distinctive style: clean white Fred Perry under a long green parka, and a wool beret, bought during his first trip to Mundaka (a renowned and dangerous surf spot in the Basque Country). Guancia combed his hair perfectly and managed his stubble immaculately. He inspired all the local skaters and surfers with his left wing and socialist political opinions.

Guancia was the best at wave forecasting. As soon as an afternoon easterly breeze turned to the north a few degrees, he would head to the marina bar, order a 75cl bottle of Moretti (Italy's cheapest beer), and collect first-hand information on the conditions out at sea from the fishermen. Then he'd strap his red 9'4" (shaped in the 1960s by Californian legend Sonny Vardeman) and blue 6'6" (shaped in the early 1980s by equally legendary Californians the Campbell brothers, inventors of the three-finned bonzer a decade before the thruster) to the roof of a red 1976 VW Beetle and drive full speed along the 2.8 km long harbour wall, all the way to the beacon. My good friend Emiliano Mazzoni and myself would often cram into his back seat. He loved to scare us kids with stories of shipwrecks and failed rescues, performed right there, in huge breaking waves, under the *capanni*.

"That's where private Terzo Sirotti lost his life," Guancia would say passing by a little column erected on the first section of the pier by the mourning family. The shrine was adorned with plastic roses and a sepia portrait of a young Terzo Sirotti. "It was a huge Bora in December '66," added Guancia. "Their boat had missed the entrance and capsized. Terzo rescued a dozen people. Then went down like a stone, right there, in the outgoing rip, never to be found again." Once at the beacon, Guancia would get out of the car, light a Lucky Strike, inhale, exhale, open a black note-book and start his divination, pencil in hand, cigarette in mouth. He'd smell the breeze between smokes, count seconds between passing waves, note cloud direction, shape and colour, even re-mark on bird trajectory. "Ducks hate flying downwind. You guys know that? It ruffles their feathers and makes it uncomfortable for them to steer. So they fly back to the marshes before Bora gets too strong. Would you enjoy surfing with a stick up your ass? Same principle, but they know it in advance." We'd lough out loud, nervously, sometimes scared by his dark humour.

Before leaving at sunset Guancia would sum up his notes and announce a verdict. "Wind has turned 15 degrees to the north-east, period has jumped from 3 to 6 seconds, ducks came in way before sunset, and all military boats have anchored facing out. Wax up your boards kids, we'll be surfing tomorrow."

At night we'd watch re-runs of John Milius' Californian cult classic *Big Wednesday* (1978) on VHS. It was a big hit for the small surf scene in Italy and we even learned to shape surfboards from watching it. Of course we studied the moves. When the swell was up goofyfoot Guancia would ride his shortboard as if Hawaiian Gerry Lopez from the closing *Big Wednesday* sequences. But when it was small he was a master on his longboard. He'd studied the moves of Billy Hamilton (who played the surfing sequences for the character Matt Johnson in *Big Wednesday*) to perfection. Guancia had a narrow stance, front-side on Marina di Ravenna's long left, connecting sections with cross-stepping and rollercoaster turns. But often he was still, just in trim, minimalist. He had an almost telepathic awareness of the waves, always on the best set.

We would snag a few rides on Guancia's longboard, but we were all hardcore skaters, and shortboarding was our domain. Guan-cia would always shout at us if we flapped and hopped around

too much, demanding, "Keep it smooth boys. Style is everything."
And we surfed every swell until every wave disappeared, then skated parks and ramps and streets when it was flat. Then, when the summer holiday of 1988 ended I moved my skateboard and my books into a 16th century building in Venice, travelling back down the coast to Ravenna at any sign of swell, and usually bringing Guancia (who had a passion for left wing socialist governments as well as lefthanders) the odd bit of Maoist paraphernalia I got second-hand from older students who had already travelled to China. Bit by bit, I was starting my journey east as if caught in a magnetic field.

CHAPTER THREE

VENETIAN PROPHECIES

I was heading into central Venice on the front-row of public boat number one, passing through the last section of Venice's Grand Canal at noon. Fierce gusts of unseasonably cold Bora wind started to wipe the sky clear of clouds, revealing a vivid cobalt. The dome of Santa Maria Della Salute, and the triangular Punta Della Dogana - both carved out of white Istrian stone - offered a warm glow as the overcrowded *vaporetto* approached San Marco Square. This place welcomes 22 million tourists per year, but every stone, every reflex here is about 'going' not 'coming'. While in America it was 'go West', from Venice east was the suggested direction, following in the footsteps of Marco Polo.

My surname, Zanella, is typically Venetian, but I don't belong to this wealthy city. My ancestors left Venice in the so-called '*La Serenìsima Republica*' in the late 18th century. I don't know what pushed them to leave this open-air museum. It may have been the economic depression caused by the waning Venetian monopoly on Mediterranean commerce; or one of the plague outbreaks that decimated the population. But suddenly - spying through arched windows of tiled multi-coloured glass to look inside the private palaces along the Grand Canal, filled with Rococò Murano chandeliers - I regretted our family departure from the city. 'We' left this behind and moved south to farm the fertile lands between the Adige and Po rivers, and never looked back.

Venetians called families like mine 'zappalotti', a derogatory term meaning 'those who dig soil'. They caricatured us as having callous hands, big shoes and narrow minds. At least, this time, I wasn't a tourist. Last time I was here, with my parents, we paid a fortune for a defrosted pizza, purchased blown glass from Murano at a ridiculous price, and bought a plastic gondola (the local asymmetric rowing boat) with red blinking LEDs, emblazoned with 'made in Taiwan' across the hull. That was the early 1980s, and the world's production of plastic gadgets had not yet moved to mainland Communist China.

Today it was different: this was the first day of my future - a future that, for the first time, in my 19 years, I had chosen. 'Zappalotti', but on a mission.

On the main bend of the Grand Canal, just down from Rialto Bridge, I arrived at Ca' Foscari, Italy's leading University in the field of foreign languages, housed in an intimidating 15th century four-floored Gothic castle. This imposing structure once belonged to the longest reigning Duke of Venice, Doge Francesco Foscari (1373-1457). Ca' Foscari was one of the few Universities in the late 1980s to offer Sinology, the branch of linguistic studies specialising in China and its culture. But the enrolment queue was a lot shorter than the department of Yamatology (Japanese studies) that had over one hundred students anxiously lined up in front of the secretary. I paid the annual fee, presented all my paperwork, including the compulsory typhoid vaccination certificate, and enrolled as a freshman at the Department of Oriental Studies. Now it was time to go and see some sights.

I wanted to catch a glimpse of the Adriatic from atop the Campanile di San Marco (San Marco bell tower). As I turned the south corner of the tower, 90 meters high, I got hit by a very recognisable smell of dry continental landmass: Bora. I knew the surf would be pumping in Ravenna. The northeasterly Bora smelled different than Ravenna. It had the scent of foliage, likely from the karst slopes of Istria, 70 km upwind, and the aftertaste of clams decomposing at low tide, probably picked up on the eastern mud banks of Torcello. It was late summer, and Bora had showed up unexpectedly, like a traveller returning home. Had I been watching I might have witnessed the proceeding lightning storms on the horizon, typical across the Dalmatian coast. My antennae were up and fully tuned.

From the top of the bell tower I leaned over the balcony. I was nervous, feeling an urge to jump back on the boat, then the train, head home and surf. But then my eyes were drawn eastward, across a carpet of red tiled roofs dotted with flowery verandas, towards the island of San Giorgio and its white marble, then the verdant green of Le Vignole and Sant'Erasmo, all the way to Lido, the last island separating the internal lagoon from the open waters of the Adriatic. I couldn't spot any waves. There's no surf in Venice. It's too far north to receive any decent northeast swell. But the panorama was incredible, spanning hundreds of kilometres, from the Alps in the north to the low lying planes of the Adige River in the south. Fantasies of the distant surf were displaced by the realities of living history.

While there were no waves in sight, the signs of the rippling Silk Road were everywhere: the cathedrals, the Byzantine domes, the marble horses, all radiated influences from the east - Constantinople, Damascus, Samarkand, and Hangzhou of the Song dynasty. One thousand years of exploration were presented, carved onto Gothic pillars, framed into gilt mosaic and preserved in the local dialect. Venetians even have their own language, replete with influences from the east, and distinctive for turning most 'a's into 'e's, generating a melodic sound, like a properly tuned viola. I surfed a historical fancy, placing myself back in the 15th and 16th centuries.

Later that day I collected the keys for a flat in Sestrier Castello, a 20 minutes walk from the Chinese Department. The building, Palazzo Tetta, was designed by the great sculptor and architect Jacopo Sansovino (1486-1570) and owned by the notorious Colombo family. They were rich merchants who, unlike my ancestors, never left town and got even richer when everyone else moved out. After World War Two, when Venice's population started to drop, the Colombo family bought a dozen palaces for a fistful of liras, ensuring prosperity for generations to come.

At the start of every month I'd meet Madame Colombo on the so-called 'noble floor' (the first) - just under the 'service floor' I shared with other student tenants - to pay the one million lira monthly rent. A maid in an azure uniform would open the door and Madame Colombo, or *La Signora,* would meet me in her studio, count every bill, then hand me a receipt, normally exchanging a few stories about the house, or her Welsh Corgi dog named Ramses, apparently direct from Queen Elizabeth's farm in Pembrokeshire. "The palace has seen plenty of characters," said *La Signora.* "In the late 16th century it served as a brothel for homosexuals. Prostitutes would show their breast (*tetta*) at the windows, luring passing gondolas." Venice's central government was so homophobic that they beheaded or burned anyone caught in the act.

Palazzo Tetta, surrounded by canals on three sides, is one of the few island-houses in Venice. From behind, at Ponte Conzafelzi, it vaguely resembles a battered Spanish galleon at a busy dock, its slim symmetrical stern waiting to be repaired, stocked up and sent back to sea. Venice is built on water, yet most Venetians have no confidence at all with the open sea. They are, on the contrary, formidable walkers. Public transportation is intermittent and expensive, shuttling tourists up and down the Grand Canal and leaving vital parts of the city un-served. Few locals own a boat, and end up relying on their own steam, traversing slippery marble, frigid winters and the frequent *acqua alta* (high water). At every noticeable swell, the low-lying parts of town flooded with brackish water from the canals. The surge, at times over one metre, is triggered by strong winds, high tides, and the limited capacity of the shallow northern Adriatic to absorb water. When the tide reached a certain level, a siren announced the coming flood and public offices closed, roadside shops raised barricades, and everyone wore rubber boots. Tourists inadvertently splashed in sewers, got stuck in restaurants, or paid to be ferried through flooded streets on hand pushed trolleys called *caretti*.

The biggest challenge in Venice was finding my way around. The city is a labyrinth spanning four kilometres in length and two and a half kilometres in width. Miss a turn and you end up in the opposite side of town. The number of crossroads is so high that giving or receiving directions is totally useless. Venetians bump into lost foreigners daily. They have been doing this for over 1,000 years. Consequently, they have evolved a little performance for the moment someone asks, '*Scusi, per Rialto?*' They look around as if sensing magnetic north, then scratch their heads, point arm and finger in the particular direction and say, '*de'à*' (in that direction). The tourist is generally none-the-wiser.

The last thing I wanted to do was get tangled up with the hordes of tourists next to landmarks at Rialto and San Marco. Here the tourists walked in groups, occupied whole alleyways and stopped atop every bridge. Not only did they slow pedestrian traffic, but they also left a visible trail of empty water bottles and food packaging. In my eyes this was mass tourism at its worse, a far cry from supporting sustainability, a curiosity for details, and communication with locals.

I didn't meet any tourists along the 'locals-only' zones of the Jewish Ghetto, Fondamenta Nuove, or in Campo Santa Maria Formosa. Here the walking rules were strict, and the hand-pushed *caretti* trolleys dominated. These two metres long chariots can carry anything, from flowers to photocopy machines to people, up and down bridges and around narrow corners. Everything you eat, drink or simply use in Venice is first shipped in on a nine metres diesel barge named a '*mototopo*' (motor mouse), then loaded onto *caretti* and hand pushed to the final destination. Venice's lowest working class, who speak in a proud dialect, traditionally operate *caretti*. As they approached, moving at twice your speed, they would scream: '*Vara e gambe*' (watch out for your legs) to men, or simply '*nylon*' to women. Such warnings were essential or else your lower limbs (or nylon socks, stockings or tights) would be whisked away by two iron bars. It's a deadly weapon and with most *calli* (Venetian for streets) being only two metres wide, collisions were common.

After a few weeks, multiple wrong turns and several bruised shins, I had learned three separate routes to the Chinese Department. Importantly, I got used to the rules: walk fast, stick to the right side, don't stop on top of bridges, and don't use earphones. A favourite route was across Ponte dei Pugni bridge via the bookstore in Santa Margherita. There was a green barge that sold the freshest vegetables in the area - big purple artichokes and ruby *radicchio* harvested that same morning on the northern island of Torcello. There are over 300 bridges in Venice. Each one has a sound, a smell and a story. Some mark a border between historically conflicting districts. For example, Ponte dei Pugni (the Bridge of Fists) near San Barnaba, divides the eastern *Castellani* and western *Nicolotti* - proud rivals since the 8th century. The very word 'ghetto', so widely used in hip hop and rap culture, is Venetian. Ponte dei Pugni divides the eastside men, who historically wore red, and the westside, who wore black. Women from the east broached a small bouquet on the left of their blouse, while those from the west wore it on the right.

Disputes were solved through fist-fights on the bridge. Some would turn into bloody *vendettas* with up to 300 people involved, spectators cheering from windows and rooftops. I found an old book in Santa Margherita called *Artistic Views of Venice* that included a 1673 painting of such a fight by Joseph Heintz the Younger (1600-1679) who was from Germany, but had settled in Venice. Most buildings were still identical, and so were the two bell towers of Angelo Raffaele, one of the oldest churches in the city piercing the clouds in the background. Clothing fashions may have changed, gondolas had lost their roofed cabins and most windows were now closed, but the vibrancy of Venice, the people, the factionalism, the curiosity, the anxiety, the pace, the sounds were the same. It felt like a fist-fight could still erupt at any moment. Unlike Ravenna, stuck in an 'oriental anxiety', Venice was alive and kicking.

The library of the Chinese Department was on the first floor of Ca' Cappello, a sturdy palace overlooking Campo San Polo, Venice's biggest open space after San Marco. Dotted with trees and benches, Campo San Polo was a hangout for Venetian families, especially in the autumn when they enjoyed the last warm afternoons before the long freezing winters. Kids chased each other on pushbikes, mums sipped espressos at the cafes, and dads followed live football on the radio, often competing with the cries of circling seagulls.

Although San Polo is Venetian for Saint Paul, Campo San Polo to me felt like an ode to the great Marco Polo (1254-1324). He was the mighty Venetian merchant, explorer and writer, and the first European to leave detailed chronicles of travelling to China. One paper I looked forward to in the first year was dedicated to the history of exploration, and *Il Milione (The Million* or *Book of the Marvels of the World)* was the main topic. This was the 13th century travelogue written down by Rustichello da Pisa from the tales told by Marco Polo from his travels through Asia between 1271 and 1295. And it was this book that inspired Italian Christopher Columbus and many other explorers and cartographers to set sail and explore, imagining that they could open a sea route to the East.

With the adventurous spirit of Marco Polo I attended the opening of the Mandarin course at the University's Ca' Dolfin, a small Rococò palace, with a magnificent fresco by the prolific Venetian painter and printmaker Giambattista Tiepolo (1696-1770). But the first words spoken by the Head of Department, Professor Sabattini, dressed in a black Armani suit, and already dripping with sweat, sounded more like a curse than an ode to the East.

"I've noticed over 70 of you chose Mandarin as your major this year," he said. "That's a record for our department and I have to thank you all for your trust. Still, I must warn you. You will never make a career out of Chinese studies."

I was, to say the least, confused by this pessimism - a setting rather than a rising sun so early in the course, the curtain dropping. Several mirrors framed in gold leafed stuccos mercilessly caught and reflected the image of Professor Sabattini's mouthing in painfully slow speech. In-between fabricated smiles he slid his hand under his white starched collar, undid two neck buttons, and loosened his crimson tie, offsetting the stifling formality of the suit, however well tailored. To round off the pessimism, he added: "And if you're hoping to find a job here at the department," pausing to present a condescending wink to the other lecturers at the table, "Well, you'd better forget it as, unluckily, we are all at least 20 years from retirement." The teachers smiled reassuringly. Maybe we should all Go West?

Even Frenchman Napoleon Bonaparte was more optimistic about China than Professor Sabattini. In 1803, before becoming

Emperor, he apparently pointed at China on a map and said, 'Here lies a sleeping giant. Let him sleep for when he wakes up, it will shock the world.' He had read extracts from Confucius' *Analects*, translated by the Italian Jesuit Matteo Ricci in the late 16th century. Chinese philosopher Confucius claimed national welfare was achieved through the moral cultivation of its people, particularly the leaders, based around good education and virtue or respect for others and their particular roles in society. Confucius had a huge influence on China and the Chinese education system in particular. In contrast to the 'wild man' in Daoism that celebrated the dark outliers of nature, Confucianism focused on civility, manners and public decency. Our lecturers had grown up studying in government Universities, right under the watchful eye of Mao Zedong and Zhongnan Hai, the controlling bureaucratic district in Beijing. But this was now 1988. The new leader Deng Xiaoping had been changing the face of the country, dismantling the basic bricks of Maoism. He had shut down People's Communes in 1983, allowing farmers to sell their products privately, and pushed hard for technological and economic development in the 'open door' policy. *Coca Cola* had opened its first Chinese plant. The newly developed Special Economic Zones, where foreign companies could invest, were the engine behind what the world media would call 'the Chinese miracle'.

Professor Sabattini sat down and each lecturer stood up in turn to introduce their course: Language (written and spoken), History (from 5000 BC to 1911), Literature, Philosophies of the Far East, History of Exploration and Chinese Art were the mandatory papers in year one. And, despite his caustic speech, I would quickly learn to love Professor Sabattini's book on Chinese History, no doubt written while buckled up in his black Armani suit.

Thankfully the event was over in half an hour. And I was not fazed by the pessimism. I had learned to ignore what didn't interest me at Liceo Roiti in Ferrara, and in Venice I had already spoken to the older students who had spent several semesters in China, and had a less conservative perspective than the lecturers. "China is changing fast," said the older students. "Young people listen to rock and roll and smoke weed. There's less bikes and more cars and new opportunities." These older students, some well into their thirties, were a curious array of characters. They included smartly dressed art collectors importing antiquities from Panjiayuan market in Beijing, and learning the language in the process. These clever thieves had proven Professor Sabattini wrong as Deng Xiaoping had started transforming the Communist economy.

Located on the southern suburb of the capital, around the third ring, Panjiayuan market now covers an area of 50 thousand square metres with over 4,000 shops and stalls clustered under a highway bridge. In the late 1980s it was still a spontaneous gathering of farmers, coming to town to sell what they had dug out of their newly privatised fields. And this didn't stop at potatoes, carrots and white cabbage. Skilfully carved and hugely valuable ritual jade disks used by shamans during the so-called Spring and Autumn period (771-476 BC), and opalescent porcelain from the Song dynasty (960-1279) and Ming dynasty (1368-1644) were hidden under piles of vegetables. The older students told me that smuggling such treasures out of the country was simple: buy a similar (and of course fake) remake of the object from one of the authorised art stores in Beijing, keep the receipt, throw away the worthless object, and bring the Panjiayuan original (with receipt of 'purchase') into Europe. At the arrival airport in Malpensa, Milan, their hard-to-obtain long-term visa would infer that they were students, forced to spend months in a repressive Communist country, coming home replete with a nice gift for the family. Some of these souvenirs ended up being sold at world famous auctions and displayed in museums. Others drifted undetected into private collections.

Trust assured, all the older students believed in Napoleon's prophecy. The future looked bright. Europeans were opening commercial routes, starting joint ventures and fulfilling Deng Xiaoping's aphorism 'to get rich is glorious', with huge private companies now allowed to do business. Change was in the air and I could not wait to experience it. I was soon spending every day at the Chinese Department, mumbling the first syllables of what would become my second language: Mandarin. And of course, the cultural treasures of studying Chinese extended far beyond learning the language. Tea drinking was essential. I loved the *pu'er* from Yunnan, but also developed a penchant for powdered green tea whipped to a perfect froth and reputed to be the closest you could get to a legendary Song dynasty tea. It is milky in texture, pea green in colour, tastes like cannabis and milk froth, and leaves a brilliant aftertaste of bubbles fizzing on your tongue, all thanks to the low brewing temperature. Sipping this from a 12th century purple ceramic cup from the imperial kiln (smuggled out of Beijing) while reading and listening to gondola singers in Venice was the soundtrack to my studies.

CHAPTER FOUR

CHINESE CHARACTERS

I very quickly found out that the main difficulty with learning Chinese is pronunciation. Chinese is a tonal language where one word has many meanings dependent on the pronunciation and intonation. There are around 300 syllables, but to the non-initiated, they all sound the same. In fact, 'Chinese' is synonymous with 'incomprehensible' for many Europeans. And for good reason: 26 letters can be combined in an infinite number of speakable words, all differing in length and sound. Linguists explain that modern Chinese uses an increasingly smaller portion of the original sounds. This generates a massive need for 'tone' to bring variety to all this apparent uniformity.

Mandarin (the official state language) and Cantonese (spoken in Hong Kong, Macau, the Guangdong province and most British and American Chinese communities who originally came from these areas) are the two main dialects of the Chinese language. Mandarin has four tones. Cantonese has six. When starting to learn Chinese, not only do you have to memorise words that sound like nothing you've heard before, but you also have to remember what tone to apply. Is it the high flat first tone? Or is it the fourth descending one? A classic example is the word '*ma*', which can mean 'mother' (妈 *mā* first tone), 'horse' (马 *mǎ* third tone), 'fuck off' (骂 *mà* fourth tone) or be used as a question mark (吗 *ma* neutral tone). Fail to hit the right tone and the sentence is turned upside down, inside out, or you are slapped in the face for telling someone's 'mother' to 'fuck off'!

An important foundation for me was reading a book by American sinologist John DeFrancis called *The Chinese Language: Fact and Fantasy*. DeFrancis estimates that it takes seven to eight years for a Mandarin speaker to learn and master three thousand words, whereas French and Spanish language learners can reach the same level in half that time. And this is just for speaking. Writing is a whole other world.

The aura around written Chinese characters among the Sinology students was indisputable. They are elegant, complex and fascinating. But mastering them is a lifelong commitment. Older students had a game that inferred how hard it was to break into this written code. They'd pick up one random book from the library, put 1,000 liras each on the desk, and see who could read and translate just the title. Winner takes all. Sometimes they went for three of four books before somebody won.

"You only need to remember 2,000 characters to read a newspaper," said the lecturers, downplaying the difficulties. My fellow students and I felt it was an impossible task and almost one third of freshmen quit before the end of the first semester. Yes, there are about 2,000 'basic' characters that you cannot ignore. But the interesting ones are more complicated, and often constitute the core meaning in a sentence.

Of all the characters who regularly scaled the Chinese Department's pink marble stairs, the 'translation geeks' were the most intriguing. They were commonly too shy to partake in the evening aperitif and stayed in the library until late. Mr Scarpari, an eminent sinologist who specialised in traditional Chinese (古文 *gǔwén*), carefully selected them to carry out detailed linguistic tasks. Their job would be to bisect the grammar and philology of one specific text, all the way to the very deepest details. Many of them spent their entire university years on one single character, such as 'virtue', in one single text, such as the Confucian Analects. They started translating the latest uses of the character, comparing it with previous translations, then went on counting how many times that character had been used as a verb, an object, a complement and so on. There was something both miserable and sublime about their task. Miserable because they unknowingly constituted the brute work behind more noble projects, doing all the time-consuming research our lecturers needed to support their publications. Sublime because their boring essays were then catalogued and put at the disposal of the world of sinologists and students, a web of university lecturers, publications and institutions, trying to cast light on China's 5,000 years of literary history. I quickly released that 'translation geeks' were the unsung heroes, the working force behind cultural exchange and ground-breaking books in history, science, philosophy and literature, accredited to their mentors.

Translating, the noble act of transferring written information from one language to another, is a serious challenge. The work gets harder as the distance between the two cultures increases. Latin to English is not that far considering at least 30 percent of words have uses in common, such as 'persona', 'salt' or 'geography'. These are fossilised words inherited from the *lingua franca* of the Roman Empire and modernised into English.

There are no such shortcuts when dealing with traditional Chinese, the official language of dynastic China. While modern Chinese is universally recognised as a hard language, the classical Chinese that 'translation geeks' were dealing with is near impossible. Translating word by word, and applying grammar schemes is not enough. Passages can only be fully understood and translated with someone competently monitoring and tutoring each step of the work.

Bridging classical Chinese with a coherent translation is a slow, painful and often discomforting process, requiring endless hours with grammar books and dictionaries. There are a whole host of dictionaries: ones for simplified characters used in Communist China, ones with the traditional characters used in Taiwan and Hong Kong, and many more. There are dictionaries for grammar, dictionaries of Beijing dialect, dictionaries of proverbs, dictionaries of Chinese Communist terms, of Daoist terms, of engineering and electrical terms. The list goes on. Searching for one particular word could require a whole afternoon and half a dozen dictionaries.

In the pre-digital world, a translation session started with *The Mathews*, a 1,226 page Chinese English dictionary using a system developed by Sir Robert Henry Mathews (1877-1970), who was an Australian missionary who arrived in China in 1906 and compiled this dictionary on behalf of the China Inland Mission, a Christian Protestant society based in Singapore. Mathews was their secret weapon, a linguistics master who could crack the code of dynastic literature, break into China and inspire Christian beliefs. Mathews based his phonetics on the work of sinologists Sir Thomas Wade (1818-1895) and Herbert Giles (1845-1935), English diplomats and first professors of Chinese at Cambridge University in the late 1800s. They were the first to standardise the translation of Chinese characters into English in the late 19th century. But so-called Wade-Giles phonetics is different from the functional Pinyin used since the 1970s. Pinyin literally translates into 'spell sound' and is a much simpler way of spelling out Chinese characters with letters from the English alphabet based on their pronunciation. But most of the classic terms have only been translated using the Wade-Giles system.

A single character can require up to ten minutes to be identified in *The Mathews*. There is no alphabetic order. Each word is classified though 214 recurring components - called 'radicals' - that help to infer the meaning of the character. For example, all concepts related to water, like 'wave' (浪 *làng*), 'tide' (潮 *cháo*) or 'washing' (洗 *xǐ*) share the same radical, 氵 called 'three water drops', classified in the same section of the dictionary. To identify them implies recognising which part of the character constitutes the radical, then counting the remaining strokes inside the given character. For example 'tide' (潮 *cháo*) can be found in the section dedicated to all words containing the 'water' radical 氵 and counting 12 strokes. Already confused? And when you finally find your word in the dictionary, there will be at least ten different interpretations of that very word, all written in a language that might ring true to a Christian missionary in the early 1900s, but few people today. It was a painful and slow learning curve. And this was just for reading.

Handwriting, preferably with a brush, is the best way to deepen your learning experience of Chinese. The high art of handwriting is Chinese calligraphy, mixing pictograms and thousands of years of tradition, and fusing painting and meditation. A 'good hand' is synonymous with high education. Simply twisting a given style to one's own sensitivity can convey moral values, artistic background, political ideas, even emotion and personality.

Persistent writing and rewriting of characters was the only way to learn new words and phrases. And calligraphy was a chance to further my appreciation of Chinese culture. So I decided to take private calligraphy lessons from the already legendary (among older students) Professor Yang, a slender lecturer in his late 40s. He was an expert in literature sent from the prestigious Beijing University (or Beida) to assist students writing their final year thesis, and offered private two hours long lessons at his studio apartment for 30,000 liras. Professor Yang was renowned among fellow lecturers for three things: his impeccable calligraphy brushwork, his background in 太极 *Tàijí* martial arts, and his devotion to an ancient Daoist meditation and healing technique known as 氣功 *Qigong*. According to Comrade Zhao, the head lecturer who organised the private lessons, Professor Yang had healed himself from liver cancer through *Qigong*, a practice that enhances energy circulation around internal organs by breathing techniques and hyper-slow movements.

"When he was younger and living in Beijing," said Comrade Zhao before my first lesson, "he was a fighter of the *Taiji* martial art known as *Bajiquan,* defending his friends and relatives when needed. After someone had attacked his brother, he found the culprit, and with just two moves put him to the floor. The culprit stayed unconscious for half an hour, then woke up and apologised. He doesn't use the so-called *baofa* 'explosive power' of *Bajiquan* anymore. He saves his power for when it's needed and focuses on the control of the 氣 *Qi,* the Daoist energy." This guy, and the mysteries surrounding him, already fascinated me.

A beautiful piece of calligraphy was hanging on the front door of Professor Yang's studio on a rice paper scroll one metre high. It contained three characters, 流與空 *liú yǔ kōng* 'flowing through void', in a cursive, but clear, style. The first character 'flowing' was mechanically perfect, with the three strokes of the radical 'water' (氵) bold and slowly executed. The brushwork then become faster at the second character 'through' (與) drawn smaller, almost out of synch, as if the painter had been stalling the brush, waiting for a wave of creativity. The last character 'void' (空) had nearly been swallowed by the white sheet. It was as if the one thin uninterrupted line with five sharp turns, fading to white, had been drawn at the apex of Professor Yang's meditation. "He threw away over 20 sheets before keeping this one," whispered Comrade Zhao before we knocked at the door, apparently more concerned about the cost of rice-paper than the artistic value of the calligraphy.

流於空 *liu yu kong*
Flowing through void
Cursive script

47

Professor Yang called to come in, and Comrade Zhao led me into his Spartan studio apartment. Professor Yang was sitting at his desk, dressed in what looked like a pyjama outfit. He was scribbling on a sheet of grey paper with a small brush. His desk was empty, apart from a thermos of green tea and a cup of water. Elbow elevated, his right forearm was moving parallel to the desk as he brushed. His hand was bent upwards to hold the brush in a perpendicular grip. He was exercising the 'grass style', the quickest of cursives, with expert precision. He was using water, not ink, so the writing was visible for about ten seconds, before drying up and disappearing, as ephemeral as a breaking wave.

He finished his last stroke, lifted his head and welcomed us, "*Huanyin Huanyin* (Welcome, welcome)." Comrade Zhao introduced us, I sat down, she left, and we settled into our first lesson.

"Let me introduce you to the four treasures," started Professor Yang. He rested the brush, lifted up a brown shoebox from the floor, and slid the top open. "Brush, paper, ink stick and slab constitute the tools of the art, and it takes a good fifteen minutes of preparation before you can even handle the brush," he added. The ink was in a solid rectangular stick, the size of a cigarette lighter, embellished by gilt engravings; "It's made of pine soot," he said as I feasted on the rich resinous smell. "It must be ground by rubbing it on this small concave slab of stone, filled with a few spoons of water." The fourth treasure, the paper sheet, was unforgivingly thin and came in A4 format, containing 20 squares to offer coordinates for beginners.

We started grinding ink with a circular motion similar to the one used to apply wax on a surfboard. Professor Yang immediately corrected my sitting posture, grabbed my hand from above and accompanied it in a smooth rotating movement: "Inhale three rounds. Exhale three rounds," he said. I could smell garlic in his breath. It hovered over my head. My breathing got deeper, extending all the way to the lower abdomen.

Once the water had turned into a shiny black paste, Professor Yang pulled out two of his bigger weasel fur brushes from the brown shoebox, and we started dipping them sideways in the wet end of the ink stone until they turned soft. Unlike in the West, where the brush is commonly held at an angle by the combined pressure of index and middle finger against the thumb, Chinese calligraphy uses all five fingers and a peculiar grip on the brush, similar to a Buddhist *mudra* pose. There's little room for personal variations in grip, perhaps purposeful to standardise the process. With my wrist bent upwards, the bamboo shaft was literally engulfed in my hand, held vertical by the five contact points, from the upright thumb to the nails of the last two fingers pushing against it from underneath. The feeling was unfamiliar. And as soon as the tip touched the paper my confidence vanished.

Even the most simple line, forming 'number one' (一 *yī*) has a precise code of execution. You cannot just dip the brush and slide it from right to left. You have to draw a number eight with it, so that the energy stays within the drawing, and the character 'flows'. My first attempt at a simple pictogram 'water' (水 *shuǐ*) happened one hour into the first lesson. But it was a total wipeout. The symmetry was offset, with black smears at each corner revealing my poor control. "Your water does not flow," said Professor Yang, breaking the silence. It took about 20 attempts before I could produce something readable. But that feeling of the brush, suspended between paper and hand, gliding through empty space and leaving a visible wake, was enough to hook me for two years of classes every Monday and Thursday evening at Professor Yang's studio apartment on Lido Island.

There are eight basic 'turns' to be mastered, before you can 'surf' the sinuous expanse of calligraphy, from the simple straight line (known as 橫 *héng*) for the character 'number one', to more complicated side swipes and hooks. Like the take-off, and the bottom-turn in surfing, they constitute the foundation of every ride. The word frequently used as the starting point for lessons is 'eternity' (永 *yǒng*) because it contains all of these eight basic strokes.

My first few lessons were spent practicing 'eternity' until a single effort produced fluid and solid lines and dots. Then we moved to the Daoist milestone, Laozi's *Dao De Jing*. The frequent use of repetition and juxtaposition make it ideal for calligraphy lessons and for linguistic rehearsal. We spent a whole winter copying the first five chapters, first in the so-called Regular script, then in the elegant Small Seals script (also known as the Bronze script) of the 3rd century BC, when Chinese language was first standardised. But we also discussed the meaning of the text, and the ancient Chinese philosophy of 陰 *yīn* 'shady side' and 陽 *yáng* 'sunny side', that describe how opposite forces become interdependent in nature, influencing both Confucianism and Daoism. Even 'airhead' surfers know the *yin* and *yang* symbol, adopted by *Town and Country Surfboards* in Hawaii since 1971. I started to understand the Laozi quote I wrote into the poster on my bedroom wall at home in Ferrara all those years ago.

I drew immediate parallels between surfing and calligraphy. Weasel fur is famous for its elasticity. It performs like a long flexible single fin. The ink-soaked tip holds a perfect straight line in trim, but change direction (like pushing into a deep bottom-turn on an overhead wave), and it explodes in radical controlled hooks. The line can be thin and fast, as if avoiding a falling lip, then become thick and heavy, compressing up and down in narrow rail-to-rail arcs. Like a surfer on a wave, ink gives meaning to the media it traverses, and feeds off the space on a page.

I soon got to know Professor Yang pretty well. He was financially broke, his calligraphy equipment the most expensive thing he owned. He joked about only being able to afford cheap jasmine tea. "A good Jasmine tea in Beijing," he'd say after pouring a cup from his thermos flask, "will be alive with the flavour of the flowers, and not made of big broken leaves like this stuff I drink here." He couldn't afford anything better. His 500 thousand liras monthly pay (equivalent to 250 Euros) was way too low to rent anything in central Venice. So, he lived on Malamocco, the southern tip of Lido Island, in a cheap compound overlooking a wind battered stretch of Adriatic coast, over one hour away from the Chinese Department. Erosion had destroyed the beach. All you could see north and south was silty water splashing on 'murazzi', an endless procession of jetties and breakwaters intended to defend the narrow island from the surges of the Adriatic.

In the middle of our two-hour lesson, Professor Yang would open the terrace and face the freezing Bora wind for a few minutes. He would rise tall, spread his arms, open his hands, inhale cold air through his nose, and exhale in short breaths, producing a flute-like sound. He would return into the studio with boiling hot hands. He said that he could absorb his *Qi*, or energy, as Daoists call it, from wind, trees, rain, open spaces, or simply by rinsing his hands under a running tap of water. He could awaken his *Qi* in his brain, and lower it down to the abdomen, the 丹田 *dāntián*, then start his *Qigong* practice. The *dantian* (also known as the 'pillar field') is where he explained that he could store his *Qi*. This spot is also recognised by acupuncture as a vital meridian. Then he could use his *Qi* for the creative act of writing, the movement of *Taiji*, or for internal self-healing.

I soon learned that the particular type of *Qigong* Professor Yang practiced was called *Hunyuan Taiji*. "When everything is spinning, it's *Hunyuan*," he said. "It symbolises the orbital path of the sun, the moon, the constellations, the Earth... when everything is moving together. In our own body there is circulation of *Qi* and blood, and they follow particular meridians. For example, up the inner leg and down the outer side; same thing with the arms. When everything is circulating and spinning together, this is *Hunyuan*. *Hunyuan Taiji* helps us control our spinning *Qi*."

Professor Yang enjoyed listening to me talking about surfing, so one day I came to the lesson with some surf magazines. He was immediately enchanted. "Waves are the cleanest and most obvious representation of *Qi* on the planet," he claimed. "They circulate, morphing from *yang* to *yin* constantly, and repeat a circle without ever being identical." "What do you think of the surfers riding the waves?" I asked, as he leafed through the magazine. "The surfers are over exposed to the *yang* power of water. Water is *yin* only when it is still. As it breaks and turns into foam, it becomes *yang*. So, surfers are constantly into a *yang* environment and should practice *Taiji* to balance that. If we don't find a way to balance all that *yang* we may become violent or start using drugs."

Professor Yang came to a photo spread of a group of surfers sitting on their boards waiting for waves. "Here is the *yang*. It's like they wait for the moment, the *Qi*, as if waiting for an important person. Waves are not there all the time. They are precious gifts from nature." "And what do you think of this?" I asked, turning the page to a centrefold of a huge tube, the rider locked inside a monster blue barrel. "This the perfect example of stillness in-action," he said. "We call it *wuwei*".

Professor Yang gave me a Chinese name - 李健豪 *Lǐ Jiànháo*. The surname 'Li', for my love of the Tang dynasty poet and calligrapher Li Bai (701-762) who famously drowned on the Yangtze

River while trying to embrace the reflection of the moon, and the first name 'Jianhao' meaning 'valiant hero', for my love of surfing. The Tang is considered the golden age of Chinese poetry, and Li Bai one of the greats, writing about travel, landscape, the futility of wars that seemed to be an ever-present part of Chinese history, his love of alcohol and his empathy for the common person. Above all, Li Bai's poems were odes to Daoism, and the relationship between people and nature. Professor Yang was also a huge fan of Li Bai, and we often transcribed his poetry.

In two years of lessons I got used to Professor Yang's *Qi* and tapped into it at every possible occasion. He could grab my brush from above, and control its movements transmitting a warm vibration. All I needed to do was inhale, exhale, relax my wrist and let him take command.

Unfortunately, Professor Yang got called back to Beijing University with just one week of warning soon after he had helped me translate the introduction to my final thesis. It was so 'last minute' that I never got to hug, or even thank, him before his departure. But he left a hare brush for me with Comrade Zhao. "This one has less whip," she said. "Yang told me that you should start to write cursive." Yet without Professor Yang as a guide, I lost my confidence with the art of calligraphy. I never felt that vibration again while taking lessons from the other lecturers who volunteered to substitute for him. They were only there for the 30,000 liras pay. Professor Yang was there for his passion for the language. Consequently, my flirt with calligraphy dried up.

It was no surprise that Beida could send or substitute staff so easily. All the Chinese lecturers at our department had been carefully selected by Beijing and any breach in government agenda could be punished. Perhaps there was a fear that Professor Yang would publish some controversial work, so that's why he was called back. But there was nothing controversial about the other lecturers. Captained by Comrade Zhao, they dressed in grey suits and sported epic paraphernalia: Mao Zedong pin on the heart, Lei Feng fur hats in winter (named after one of the Communist legends of the People's Liberation Army), plus a worn out Little Red Book in their satchel.

The flavour of Communist propaganda was peppered into the course. The first year textbooks followed two imaginary Russian students named Gubo and Palanka socialising in Beijing, 'drinking tea', 'reading in the library' or 'going to the movies'. We watched the socialist epics, like Jiang Qing's *Bridge* (1949) in which workers race to build a bridge in record time singing 'Long live Chairman Mao'. In the second and third year the textbook scenarios became increasingly political, with Gubo learning about the proletarian revolution, the differences between Maoism and Marxism, and the benefits of collectivism. Of course, these textbooks reflected the core values of Beida at the time.

I travelled to Beijing a few times during the course. Beida remains one of the most prestigious Universities in China. It was established in 1898 as Imperial University of Peking to replace the historic Imperial Academy that had served as the highest institution of learning since the Sui dynasty (581-618). In 1911 theXinhai Revolution over threw China's last imperial dynasty (the Qing) and established the Republic of China(ROC). The following year Beida started adopting a more liberal model of European education rather than the memory-based methods of imperial exams. But in 1949 when Chairman Mao announced the birth of the People's Republic, Beida became aligned to the new socialist scheme.

The University campus, near the Qing dynasty's exquisite Summer Palace of lakes and gardens, had witnessed over a hundred years of social turmoil, including the Cultural Revolution (a socio-political movement between 1966 and 1976 to re-impose Maoist ideology). But it still retained the flavour of old Beijing, with gardens, alleys, pagodas, bridges, and manmade lakes. Mao himself, and Lu Xun, possibly the most influential writer in modern China, had studied here.

Students and lecturers alike were extremely proud of belonging to Beida, often living in picturesque (now extremely expensive) *hudong* houses, with dark brick walls, internal hidden gardens and shared (and smelly) outside toilets. Walking down those alleys in the 1980s was a risky business as spittoons and bedpans were often emptied at will out of the window, right into the narrow streets. Locals in the area speak a dialect known as *Beijing hua*, an old form of northern Mandarin, made more intriguing by the use of nasal sounds and uncharacteristic rolled 'r's. Most newcomers to the area quickly pick up the accent and start calling Beijing *'Beijirrrr'*.

Back in Venice the propaganda continued. "There's no new China without Communism," sang Comrade Zhao every morning before her lecture, proudly staring through the window, beyond Campo San Polo, at a far-off horizon. Lyrics were permanently written on the blackboard and we were kindly invited to learn them by heart, practicing ten minutes every day, a sentence at a time: *"The Communist Party toiled for the nation. It pointed to the road of liberation for the people. It led China towards the light,"* we sang with Comrade Zhao.

During our third year in Ca' Foscari the entire department of Sinology was organised into a 'proletarian commune'. We spent the first semester preparing a New Year costume show for the Chinese Ambassador. It was prime propaganda, directly endorsed by the Beida's highest cadres. Attendance to 15 hours of weekly rehearsal was not mandatory, but strongly advised. "You can avoid the show," said Comrade Zhao, "but you cannot avoid me not being friendly if you do so."

We learned and performed songs from Beijing Opera to Cantonese romance to the opening tune of the show *The East is Red*. From 1966 to 1976 *The East is Red* had been the song of the Red Guards as they raided the country, burning temples and art collections in a civil unrest that drastically delayed the modernisation of the country, affecting the lives of millions. The opening line reminded me of dawn surf sessions at home in Ravenna on a final day of Bora swell when the clouds of the low pressure had moved west. "*The east is red, the sun is bright,*" and the waves came in sets of three, combed by a crisp offshore breeze. Dawn can be so bright on all east coasts. At times you cannot see the waves until they are right on top of you.

China was on top of me for sure. Because of my good performance in essays and exams I had been given one of the main parts in the show. I played the role of my poetry hero, Li Bai. I was dressed in a long white toga sown out of bed-sheets, sported a fake beard and long thin moustache. My dreadlocks were popping out of a winged, black gauze hat that I picked up from a Beijing thrift market. I'll never forget the shocked look from my parents from the third row of the Santa Marta theatre: "Wasn't he an anarchist punk-rock surfer?" asked dad, secretly proud of seeing me conforming to some sort of institution after years of rebellion at Liceo Roiti.

I rehearsed for months to draw the poem 'Autumn River Song' with my brush, and sing it to the audience in Mandarin: "*The moon shimmers in green water. White herons fly through the moonlight. The young man hears a girl gathering water-chestnuts: into the night, singing, they paddle home together.*" But when the time came, all the *Qigong* magic I had experienced with Professor Yang - that feeling of unity between mind, brush and paper - dissolved. The brush felt cold, heavy and lifeless. Black blobs oozed out of the strokes at each bend. I was so tense I nearly vomited. But I managed to raise the scroll, brush blurred writing, and sing to an audience already too bored to care about my tone. The Ambassador nodded at Comrade Zhao and clapped. The audience of 500 woke up and followed. The performance was over and all I could think about for the encore was surfing.

I was passing my exams with flying colours. I also had a deal with my parents that if I got good marks, they would help fund a midwinter trip to find my surfing *Qi* on some of the best waves in Europe. The Canary Islands, with their distinctive dry weather and countless reef breaks, was a perfect destination. Here I could dry my Bora-soaked bones, prepare for the spring term, read Chinese philosophy and surf the urchin infested barrels of Isla de Los Lobos.

CHAPTER FIVE

RIDING
THE VOID

After the busy winter term at University in Venice, I travelled to the Canaries to surf. I was now finalising my graduation thesis, a dissertation on Ming dynasty philosopher, poet and calligrapher Wang Yangming (1472-1529) first introduced to me by Professor Yang. I was studying his work under the influence of the right-hander at Isla de Los Lobos, arguably Europe's best pointbreak (and at the time still a 'secret spot'), breaking on volcanic rocks, so long and predictable it constituted the perfect canvas to my first attempts at meditative surfing in general and barrel riding in particular. Peeling along an uninhabited islet just two square kilometres in area, a short crossing away from Fuerteventura's northern town Corralejo, Los Lobos' circular waves were clearly visible from the harbour, a short bicycle ride from my rented flat.

My routine was simple: I would check the surf several times a day, any time the swell became too big for nearby breaks called The Bubble and El Hierro, the usual spots on the north coast. And if there was a big enough swell for Los Lobos, I would board the 5.00 pm ferry and set up camp (now forbidden) at Playa de la Concha, a sandy beach sheltered from the slicing northeast wind and from the many falling rocks rolling down the huge imposing volcano. Then surf the following day.

Synchronising my work with the water level was essential. Low tide, when rides were shorter and less predictable, was for translation work on my graduation thesis. At high tide *The Mathews* dictionary lay dormant on top of my inflatable sleeping mat. It was time for action. At the foot of the red caldera, billows stacked to the horizon with majestic sets of seven lines. Front lit by the rising sun, each set formed a fan, with its apex at the northern tip of the island and its rays extending for over 500 metres, all the way to my tent. It was like a white corduroy under a dark blue sky. It was the purest form of *Qi* I had ever encountered.

These Atlantic westerly swells did not bring any exotic scent because of the long distance from the closest land mass they came from: Florida, New England, maybe the Azores, days upwind on the Gulf Stream. So they just smelt like fresh oysters or mullet. This was pure ocean swell eager to swallow me alive. I would look straight into the hollow part of the waves while sipping instant coffee in my tent. It was shaped as a black *yin* and white *yang*, churning around a void in the middle, consuming time and rocks in its forward momentum. Between surfs I was reading about Wang Yangming's work on the unity of knowledge and action (知行合一 *zhī xíng héyī*), a concept shared by Daoism and Confucianism alike. Wang advocated personal morality as the main way to social wellbeing. He claimed that the fundamental root of social problems lies in the fact that one fails to gain a genuine understanding of one's self and its relation to the world, and thus fails to live up to what one could be. He also practiced a revolutionary respiration and relaxation technique called 静坐 *jìngzuò* ('quiet sitting'), evolved from Chan Buddhism and Daoism, capable of, in his own words, 'cleansing the internal mirror, and creating a state of original knowledge where intentions and deeds, reflections and actions become one.' Wang's idea of accumulating knowledge and being able to use it as a whole, by switching into an altered, intuitive state such as meditation, is similar to Socrates (470-399 BC) philosophy of 'know yourself', where knowledge and virtue coincide.

Surfing was a great way to explore Wang Yangming's massive sea of work. The ocean is an ever-changing environment. Waves are similar, but no two are identical. In sports practiced on constant playgrounds, skills can be polished through practice. But the miracle of a barrel ride requires a relationship with wave sections that might never repeat themselves in the same way. Consequently, the surfer needs to be 'one' with the wave in both a physical and a mental way. The main focus here is on void and receptivity. Daoist's call this practice *wu wei* (first introduced to me by Professor Yang) which can be translated as 'non-action' or ataraxy (a state of serene calmness). Only by emptying our minds can we create room for this leap of consciousness and become 'one' with the cosmos.

And it resonated perfectly with wave riding. All the best rides come out of a single undifferentiated effort, where all the moves you practice and plan are suddenly forgotten, linked, interiorised and adapted to an ever-changing environment. In *Instructions for Practical Living* Wang Yangming explores the relationship between man, as an agent, and nature as an ever-changing environment, explaining that, 'The sages do not consider that making no mistakes is a blessing. They believe, rather, that the great virtue of man lies in his ability to correct his mistakes and continually make a new man of himself.' This was a great philosophy for improving surfing techniques.

But there was more than just a parallel to draw to surfing in his work. Waves were a constant companion to Wang Yangming. He was from the coast of Ningbo in Zhejiang province, a town on the southern banks of the Hangzhou Bay, 200 km south of modern day Shanghai, looking directly into the Pacific Ocean. Ningbo literally means 'peaceful waves'. Similar examples pop up all along the coastline in China, maybe given as a lucky charm, meaning 'may the waves be small and the ocean merciful.' He must have seen his fair share of Pacific storms as this area receives regular swells from the winter northeasterly monsoon, the many summer typhoons crossing the South China Sea, and, most notably, from the largest tidal bore in the world affecting Hangzhou Bay at every pushing tide. Consequently, 'waves' became a great metaphor for feelings in his work.

Wang Yangming was a bureaucrat and army general, forced by senior powers to integrate hostile tribes at the outskirts of China into the empire. He advocated more peaceful methods, passionate to inspire the social morality of Confucianism. At odds with the dynastic court of the Ming, he became an outspoken and controversial figure. He was eventually imprisoned for denouncing the unjust political practices of the court. In a poem titled 'Insomnia' written in what he described as a 'ghost infested cell' where he had been locked up, Yangming compared his tumultuous feelings to a 'breaking wave' (波浪 *bōlàng*) so 'fierce' that it forced him to rethink his entire life. Among the litany of words at his disposal he picked just one term to describe the psychological state he was going through - 汹 *xiōng*. This adjective is strictly associated with dangers at sea. The left side of the character 氵 (three drops of water) restricts the use to a watery context, while its semantic part, the component 凶 *xiōng* can be translated with 'ominous', 'mighty' and 'deadly'. Its original pictographic form depicts a trap, a hole in the ground hiding two sharpened poles, a place where animals unexpectedly fall and die.

Wu Cheng'en's *Journey to the West* is also from the Ming dynasty. The author described waves a number of times. At the beginning of chapter 28 the Monkey King finally goes back to his kingdom and finds that hunters have decimated his fellow monkeys, killing most of them and destroying their forest. He is contemplating the Eastern Sea describing the waves, and uses the adjective 汹 *xiong*, just like Wang Yangming, to denote ominous surf.

When studying, making connections with things you love (for me waves and surfing) brings the learning to life and keeps the passion blazing. I was fired up by Wang Yangming, and started to consider what he would think of this ominous view at Los Lobos. How would this epiphany of *Qi*, the Daoist energy, so clean and perceivable, appeal to his sensitivity? Would he stop to meditate and absorb it? Turn it into movement and perform some *Taiji* steps? Maybe improvise some verses on a brush? Or would he ask me for a surf lesson?

Every surf was fuelled by these ideas from Chinese philosophy as I paddled back out for a set as fast as I could. Each wave had a similar pace at Los Lobos, but drew a slightly different style of the same pictogram. Bigger ones slid wide, rushing over every hole in the reef in a perfect straight line. They were easier to ride but offered less chance for a tube. Smaller, steeper waves left irregularities in their wake, a reaction to the reef, rips, rocks and bathymetry. They were the ones that turned on themselves and became hollow, producing that empty room I was desperately trying to enter and exit - the barrel.

'Empty rooms generate ghosts and demons,' read one of Wang Yangming's poems I was translating. My demons were made of wipeouts, long hold-downs, underwater lava rock sharp as knives that lacerated my wetsuit, and a fear of dwelling in that fierce empty space of the barrel. But I had the right tool for the job - a thin 6'4" shortboard shaped by Australian Nev Hyman. It had a narrow round tail, not dissimilar in shape to a big calligraphy brush. Shortboarding came to life in the late 1960s and can be considered the 'cursive script' of board riding. Shorter (mostly five to seven feet), very curved boards need more wave energy to really come alive than longboards. But once you have mastered the intricacies of their negative buoyancy, they react quickly, cutting almost to zero the time between will and action. They allow for rapid acceleration, carving tight and detailed lines, and, most importantly, taking you in and out of the barrel in the most efficient way possible (at least in theory).

The first section of the wave at Los Lobos was fairly mellow. I reacted accordingly. I could literally see the sections calling for moves, be it a long arcing top-turn, or a vertical snap. But once past a distinctive bend in the point, the wave itself asked me to abandon the safety of the shoulder, speed up and commit to the void. That was where my ghosts were taking over. I'd now been surfing for a long time, but I had limited experience of this ephemeral space that defies all definitions.

Even a fool can see that something paradoxical is happening in the barrel. The surfer is at the same time standing still, but travelling fast, completely out of the water, but engulfed in it.

Mystical explanations are inevitable when you experience it yourself. Inside the barrel sound ceases to be audible. It seems to just vibrate. And standing still, doing nothing, is the hardest possible manoeuvre. There's simply no room for intentions in this space, just for deeds. And figuring out what deeds are appropriate needs a bit of magic, a magic that was not yet happening for me.

I would drag my hand on the vertical wall and position myself, but as soon as the water went circular, my body would enter a 'speed-up' mood and accelerate away from the falling curtain, back to safety. When I forced myself deeper in the pit, stalling and slowing down, my eyes would shut, my rail would catch water, and I'd end up in a rumbling underwater rinse cycle akin to a washing machine, wave now wasted, body and board dangerously close to hitting the razor sharp lava reef bottom.

Thankfully most wipeouts were harmless. There was a feeling of suspension that could sometimes be pleasant as I was lifted up and down by the plunging wave, water among water, until I surfaced for air. But every now and then I'd have a serious wipeout, held down for tens of seconds underwater. Regardless of our bodies being constituted of 80% liquid, that experience of falling into water at speed was like crashing into a hard surface. That alone would knock the last gasp of air out of my lungs.

On these more serious wipeouts, the underwater experience was chaotic. That same creative energy, nurturing the reef, lifting plankton to the surface, was now sending me to meet my demons and fears, treating me, to use the words of Laozi in the *Dao De Jing* 'like a straw dog' (grass dogs were used for important sacrifices in pre-dynastic times). Surfers use a similar term - 'rag-dolled' - to depict what happens during wipeouts. Columns of water and trapped air would drag me around with explosive unpredictable bursts. And when the wave had passed I was still left underwater, sunk in a heavy, amniotic fluid, so thick it almost pierced my ear-drums, deafening my equilibrium, preventing me from knowing which direction was up.

In one of those numerous falls after the bend in the point, those ghosts pulled me from the empty room of the barrel, all the way to the sharp lava bottom. I hit it so hard that I nearly passed out. When I emerged, gasping for oxygen, my right leg was not responding. I pulled my leash, retrieved my board and climbed on top of it. I felt my femur-head popping back into its socket, send-ing intense pain from the hip all the way down to my right foot. The next two waves washed me closer to shore. My board was now getting severely damaged by the impact with shallow basalt, but I hung onto it, coughing water out of my lungs and trying to balance on one foot while countless urchins pierced my skin.

Thankfully another surfer came to my rescue and helped me escape the last guillotine of the shorebreak. Joe Al-roy was an excellent shortboarder from Devon in south-west England, where he worked as a lifeguard. We'd already been sharing meals whilst camping. He had just come in from the morning session, and still had his wetsuit on. "Did your back hit the reef?" he asked in a worried tone. "Yeah. I cannot feel my right leg, can't feel anything."

Joe took off my leg-rope and pushed my now finless board towards the shore for someone else to collect. He then slid both forearms under my armpits and held my chin with a pistol grip, fearing a spinal injury. He dragged me to safety. With two hours to wait until the afternoon ferry back to Corralejo, he laid me on a flat slab of rock, called his friend who had collected my board to keep my neck still, inspected my spine, tested sensitivity of my four limbs, then started to smile and make fun of the wipe-out. "Your spine is fine," said Joe, planting his ice-blue eyes into

mine. "But did you want to die kid? Didn't you hear us screaming 'NO NO' from the rocks? That wave was peeling way too close
to shore when you pulled in. That's how people get paralysed."
I hadn't heard them yelling. Inside that wave, sight and sound
had melted, then faded to black.

Joe improvised a stretcher. He took the wooden poles from
the tourist signs pointing to the beacon of Punta Martiño and to
the lagoon, and tied them together with leashes and board bags.
He carried me to the ferry with his friend singing '*Hey Ho, Hey
Ho*' from Disney's *Snow White and the Seven Dwarves* to keep my
morale up.

I arrived at the hospital, had X rays, and slowly but surely
pulled 20 urchin needles out of my feet. Four hours later the
bruise had turned deep blue and stretched across my hip. But
thankfully I hadn't broken a bone. "Take care boy. You'll surf Lobos again," were Joe's last words before heading back to his guest
house in Corralejo. Joe knew I was scared and needed encour-
agement. I felt defeated, beaten up, denied. I had never wanted
anything as bad as riding the barrel. I had spent years studying
the best in the magazines, watching videos, and visualising that
moment. But now, seconds from enlightenment, I was failing,
and didn't know why.

In the days to come I tried hard to name the ghosts I had
encountered inside that ill-fated tube, but my mind was blank.
That wipeout washed away all memories. I could visualise the
take-off, and clearly remembered how I stalled deeper than normal as the wave jacked up, but my mind could produce no record
of the few seconds I must have spent in the void. The last flash-
back was an image of the water in front of my board turning
from dark blue to yellow, as if a rock had risen up from the bottom, suddenly right in front of me.

Like the search for the eternal-life in Daoist alchemy, the art of barrel riding is an empiric process, where magic and science coexist. Board shape, fin configuration, your physical condition, everything is important but nothing, per se, suffices. No linear theory can unlock you out of this dead-end conundrum. You need an example, a spiritual guide, a strong external stimulus.

As soon as I regained my full mobility, I dropped my board to a local shaper to get fixed and I started to hang out at the atmospheric Corky's Bar next to the harbour. I hoped to meet Joe and get some advice. There was a pool table and a 'wall of fame' with pictures of epic swells. I spent an hour in front of those nicotine stained photos before Joe appeared. "How's the injury Nik?" "I can walk now, but I haven't touched water yet." I showed Joe the massive bruise around my hips. "Still scared huh?"

Joe grabbed two San Miguels, set up the pool table, and cued off. "There's definitely an equation that explains why these 15 balls have spread out the way they just did," he said. "But it's too complicated for us to grasp. We just cannot comprehend it." It was my shot. I leaned on the green velvet and set up. "Tell me," said Joe, "What's really important in this shot? Think about it." He grasped my cue with his right hand and brought me back upright. "Trajectory, and hitting angle, right?" "Wrong. It's all in the hole. We play the balls, but our goal is outside of them at the end of the ride. Focus on it, empty your mind and shoot." He let my arm go. I sipped my beer, took a deep breath, then potted the first ball, then the second. "Good job. Barrels are as simple as that. There's a million forces interacting in there, but they are too volatile and complicated. The only constant is the hole. Focus on it and you'll get spat out. If you get distracted by colours and lines, if you keep calculating angles and tangents of your board, you'll never ride it out." "I just wish it was this simple Joe.

I have no control in there. I can't even keep my eyes open. And that wipeout hasn't made it any easier. What if I hit my head?"

Joe started rubbing green chalk on the tip of the cue. "Forget about water, forget about everything that normally goes on when you surf. Just look at the shape of the barrel. If it's round, dig your arm deep and slow down. If it turns into a narrow almond, withdraw, speed up and get the hell out. In any case, look outside of it. Focus on the void."

I never really understood how to 'forget about water', lost three consecutive games of pool, and paid for three rounds of beer. But it was the best coaching fee I ever spent.

Joe's words reminded me of a passage from the *Dao De Jing* I had scribbled in Venice where Laozi illustrates his idea of a vacuum: *The reality of a room is to be found in the vacant space enclosed by the roof and the walls. Not in the walls themselves... Vacuum is all potent because it is all containing.*

I collected my fixed board and two days later the waves picked up. From the lookout on top of the fishermen's dock I could spot long lines groomed by morning offshores, linking three of the four sections at Los Lobos. It looked ominous. But I felt like I was ready to surf again. I grabbed my stuff and locked the flat. Anxiety grew when the 9.00 am ferry skirted the west side of the island. I boarded, got off at Lobos, and was soon paddling out.

My first few waves were tame. I selected smaller, softer ones and just sped down the line ahead of the whitewater, feeling out my injured joint. Then once I felt the confidence in my back leg, and endorphins started to anaesthetise the pain, I took off on a steeper one, positioned myself mid-face and took a deep breath. Right after the bend, the wave started to become more and more vertical, sending deceiving kaleidoscopic reflections to my retina and a number of sensations to the ball of my back foot. 'Forget about that, forget about that' rang out Joe's words as I focused on the dark, open void in front of me. My eyes stayed open. I was slicing through that emptiness without using a single muscle, following the morphing shape. One, three, or five seconds. I don't know how long I spent in there. But what's the difference? Every barrel is a bite of eternity. I was soon spat out into a colourful exit. I let myself sink on the board, closed my eyes and enjoyed the sweet taste of adrenalin.

At about 4.00 pm after half a dozen barrels and a few inconsequential wipeouts, I got back to the flat, totally exhausted, pain still numbed from adrenalin.

'Knowledge is the beginning of practice. Doing is the completion of knowing,' wrote Wang Yangming in *Instructions For Practical Living*. That book never got opened that day. Still, I felt I had gone deeper into my understanding of the Chinese mind on those few rides, deeper than any of the philosophy seminars I had taken so far back in Venice.

Although as students we were allowed to study Wang Yangming, sadly none of the Beijing lecturers were permitted to openly engage with his work. He was considered a radical who defied the political authority of the Ming, and his liberal idealism was banned by Beida as 'a seed of capitalism'. Consequently I had to travel to the liberal and capitalist Taiwan (where historically the Nationalists fled as the Communists gained power in the mid 20th century) to finish my translations because the work was forbidden in Beijing. But in Venice I was secretly celebrated for engaging with Wang Yangming. Deep down everyone knew you could not suppress China's history, culture and resilience of the ancestors. Daoism and Buddhism were indelibly imprinted on the Chinese population and would surely make a comeback. And since no one had translated Wang Yangming's poems in any western language before, my thesis was considered groundbreaking by the lecturers and marked by Professor Sabattini himself.

After four years of studying, countless essays, lectures, seminars, 21 exams and a dissertation, I graduated in summer of 1993 with a first-class honours degree.

CHAPTER SIX

WARTIME PERFECTION

In 1990s China was undergoing unprecedented and rapid modernisation. Italy, meanwhile, was enjoying its first surf boom, induced by increasingly accurate swell forecasts and a favourable surf industry investing money into magazines, media, events and athlete sponsorships. I was now working freelance, and felt at the forefront of both these booms, contributing to skate and surf 'zines and working as a Mandarin translator for the many Italian companies venturing into China's market. Regardless of the culture gap still separating these two worlds, China was doing a lot for my surfing, giving me the extra wealth to get to uncrowded, remote waves. With a tailored Armani suit and the latest Mac PowerBook, I was a 'beach bum' disguised as a 'cultural consultant', translating business negotiations in meeting rooms and escorting chain smoking Chinese around Italy's tourism sites.

Weeks of well-paid work were worth months of surf travel with my good friend Emiliano Mazzoni. 'Mazz' was five years younger than me, tall, broad-shouldered, permanently tanned, shy and an incredibly gifted photographer. We had been friends since high school, both hating the Italian provincial life we were born into and finding our identity through skateboarding and surfing. As teenagers we daydreamed about empty waves and had been left disappointed from traveling to the European surf Meccas, which we found overcrowded and un-adventurous. The Canaries delivered for wave quality, but lacked the buzz we were searching for.

Mazz had started studying a degree in Modern History at the University of Bologna, was focused on papers on Asia, and was the proud owner of a Canon A1. He started to put it to good use by documenting the Italian underground skate scene. We were also contributing to *SurfNews*, a black and white 32-page 'zine run by our local surf club, soon to print in full colour (myself as a writer, Mazz as a photographer). Together, we honed in on Sri Lanka and the promise of long period Indian Ocean swells. We also knew that Sri Lanka would make a great feature in *SurfNews* to help pay for the trip. Arugam Bay was the target. But after being used as a hideout by drug smuggling surfers on the 'Hippy Trail' during the 1960s and 1970s, this sleepy fishing village and its 600-metre-long pointbreak had become a no-go for surf travellers as civil war broke out in 1983 between the majority Sinhalese government and minority the Liberation Tigers of Tamil Eelam, seeking independence.

Surfing in a war zone because of uncrowded waves is something I'm not proud of. But Englishman Joe Alroy, who inspired me in the Canary Islands, had been going every season and assured me it was safe enough for a savvy traveller. Mazz and I started to research the roots of the civil conflict, traced back to English colonial times when the country was known as Ceylon. Following independence in 1948, long-running discrimination against Tamils erupted into violence by the '60s. In the late 1960s documents advocating a separate state called Tamil Eelam, in the north of the island, started to circulate. A generation disillusioned by the post-independence dream were ready to fight for a better future. In 1981 the burning of the Jaffna library and the destruction of over 90 thousand Tamil books by the ruling Sinhalese was a major turning point, inspiring extreme Tamil retaliation.

We arrived in Sri Lanka in the summer of 1996 just as the third phase of the war broke out and the conflict was more heated than ever. Nevertheless, we rented a van from Colombo airport, and crossed the Yala National Park on dirt roads. Tourism was a vital economic lifeline for many locals, so the stark realties of war appeared far removed from a lot of the country at the time. We got stoned in the van, and enjoyed the backdrop of dense palm forests and wide-open rice fields. Of course, our van was regularly searched between Colombo and Pottuvil, a town of 30,000, mainly Muslim, just inland from Aragum Bay. The intensity of checkpoints soon became a clear indicator of the hot-point conflict along the east coast. They were fully armoured outposts, with watch towers, heavy artillery, mine fields and long passport procedures.

We now knew from our driver that the territories around Tricomale and the Jaffna peninsula, further north, were totally off limits to foreigners. The troubles were starting to extend south into Ampara District, where there was a new outburst of Tamil activities - namely suicide bombings and direct attacks to Sinhalese civilians. The first glimpse of Pottuvil town was the smoking ruins of the movie theatre, destroyed by the Tamil Tigers a few days earlier. Collapsed walls and rubble were widespread, but life seemed to be continuing undisturbed, with stalls selling extra spicy *roti* and fried lentil balls filled with dried fish and fresh chilli peppers. We left the van at a bustling taxi station where a flotilla of drivers, mostly Muslim, called out the names of destinations, shuttling people to and from the nearby villages on ubiquitous three wheeled *tuk tuks* (named after the sound of their two-stroke 50cc engines). We found a driver heading to Arugam Bay, strapped our boards onto the roof and piled in the back with our bags.

The first glimpse of the coast outside of Pottuvil reminded me of the scene in Francis Ford Coppola's *Apocalypse Now* (1979) where Lieutenant Colonel Killgore (played by Robert Duvall) orders a napalm strike on the Vietnamese jungle just to enjoy 'a clean six feet swell' with a newly conscripted surf champion from Southern California. It felt as if, at any moment, helicopters blasting Richard Wagner's 'Ride of the Valkyries' would rise up from the tree-line, boards fastened to the landing bars. Kilgore's words, written by screen-writer John Milius who directed *Big Wednesday*, 'You either surf, or you fight', were resounding in my head as we handed our passports to a Sinhala officer, wrapped in a bullet-proof jacket on the last heavily guarded checkpoint on the bridge into Arugam Bay. The lagoon around it was apparently dotted with land mines and most of the food supplies, drinking water and communication lines for Arugam Bay had to come across this route. Little did we know that the line of fire between the two factions, in those months, was going to go right through this rickety bridge.

It didn't take long to discover that the once peaceful hippy community at Arugam had disappeared. Every sensible traveller had left. But there were still about 20 hardy surfers in the village, mostly Australian and European, who could not resist the now empty lineups. And the village felt safe. We immediately bought mosquito nets and rented a room with the Sirripala fishing family a short walk from the main break. The head of the family, simply known as Mama, managed the rooms, collected rent, and cooked for a handful of sun-burned red-eyed surfers. The small income earned was a financial lifeline for the family. Despite the civil unrest that surrounded us, Mama had created an idyllic place, where monkeys came to drink at the well, chickens roamed the garden, and the few local surfers would hang out after each session, discussing board design and feasting on curry, roasted mackerel, aubergines and baked potatoes.

Meanwhile there had been a flurry of suicide bombings in the main train station in central Colombo. The news didn't reach

Arugam, but was reported worldwide, and my mum waited in agony for my planned weekly call every Sunday morning, answering the phone at the first ring and reporting what she'd seen on the news. Of course, I didn't tell her about the checkpoints in force around the village, or the gun-shots, heavy artillery, watchtowers, armed guards and mine fields that surrounded us. I just said it was 'quiet and peaceful' and 'the waves were excellent'. And our routine was quite safe at the beginning. We'd surf out-front during the morning offshore winds, eat, read, during the afternoon onshore, then surf again as our bloodshot eyes enjoyed blood red sunsets and the evening glass-off. Eat. Sleep. Repeat.

The wave was out-of-this-world: long and racy, throwing barrels right to shore. Some would double up and spit out sand. But we eventually started craving different waves. We heard about Pottuvil Point, another immaculate right-hander, sheltered from the afternoon onshore, but located on the other side of the bridge. On its day it was fabled to be a longer ride than Arugam Bay. So, in spite of Mama's warning (she was Buddhist and despised the conflict), we hired a Muslim *tuk tuk* driver named Rashleem (who also seemed uninterested in the civil unrest) and ventured out, past the checkpoints on the bridge, across war-torn Pottuvil town and through a labyrinth of jungle trails that led to a pristine beach. There was not a soul in sight and the surf was exceptional. Low tide was best, with massive, groaning granite rocks marking the take-off for thrilling rides all the way to the shore.

This became our new routine. The ride took about 30 minutes and skirted the majestic Buddhist temple of Muhudu Maha Vihara. The stupas and elongated statues of this 2,000 years old monument made the landscape even more surreal, their eroded silhouettes solemnly popping out of the dry jungle as if dropped there by an alien civilisation. Dozens of buffalos gathered in the ponds, turning slowly to watch our *tuk tuk* sprint by, then turning their eyes and nostrils back to the black mud. We easily forgot about the civil war at moments like this.

The beachfront at Pottuvil Point now hosts several guesthouses and bars, but back then it was an empty Tamil Tiger controlled area, with a Revolutionary Army outpost hidden in the nearby lagoon, just inland from the wave now known as 'Whiskey'. We'd park behind the dunes, give Rashleem a bottle of water, a bag of snacks and a packet of cigarettes, and rush into the empty, perfect surf. The waves were so long and easy that our legs would burn at the end of each ride. My relationship with the barrel had improved leaps and bounds from those first attempts in the Canary Islands, and I had grown addicted to that void space and the inner calmness it produced. The waves were almost identical: take-off way outside the rock outcrop, throw a few set-up turns, then prepare for the super predictable tube washing out from a triangular rock. This slab of red granite was the fulcrum of each ride.

On our fifth trip to Pottuvil Point, we were both walking up the bay after yet another 500 metres long ride, when suddenly we met a platoon of five armed Sinhala soldiers rushing towards us. "Did you see anyone down there?" asked a soldier. "Well yes, we've seen civilians running towards the lagoon," I replied. The soldier thanked us and rushed in the direction we pointed. To be honest we were quite used to uniforms and guns by now. We actually felt safer knowing that the national army was around. But three waves later three gunshots pierced through the drumroll of the shore break. "Those were not firecrackers, right?" exclaimed Mazz. "Let's get back in the water as soon as possible. It's safer there."

On our next walk up, the platoon came back and we asked, "All good down there?" "No problem, all done, we're only shooting monkeys," answered a junior soldier.

"Quite strange for Buddhists to shoot monkeys," noted Mazz as the platoon moved away. The feeling of safety was wearing out. Half an hour went by without fire. Then all of a sudden hell broke loose just behind the dunes. The shooting this time was much closer and louder. Soon a mortar blasted in the distance. We started to panic. The Tigers had probably gotten organised and were now fighting back, defending their stronghold, ambushing the Sinhala in the scrubland. We took shelter behind the slab of red granite producing our very coveted barrel section. Soon bullets were flying overhead, and *tweezzzzzz*, one hit the rock itself, producing a piercing sound I will never forget. We lay flat on the sand, covering our heads with our boards.

"Shit Mazz, we gotta get out of here." The shooting eased and seemed to move away, so we stood up and started calling our driver Rashleem, waiting behind the sand dunes. Suddenly a platoon of about 50 units flocked the beach, M16s in hand. A senior soldier approached us and spoke from under a thick moustache. "*Majan* (the formal way to address a foreigner in Sinhalese) you've got to leave this place now. More troops are coming. There's a war going on. Do you understand this?" Rashleem appeared atop the dunes, waving his arms and screaming. He could have left us on the battle field, but he had waited. "Go now, get the hell out," demanded the senior soldier. We climbed the dunes in no time, jumped inside the *tuk tuk*, and took off, boards hanging at our sides.

As we neared the temple, the main body of the army approached. Hundreds of camouflaged soldiers were ready for battle. Rashleem rode right through them, pedal to the metal. As a patch of soft sand slowed us down, I looked straight into the eyes of a helmeted girl, loaded gun firmly grasped in her right hand. I reached my free hand out of the *tuk tuk*. She touched it and kept her dark almond eyes staring straight into mine until Rashleem found traction and the *tuk-tuk* disappeared in a cloud of dust.

I will never forget that scene: mortars, camouflage soldiers with deep worried eyes, and those perfect waves peeling off, unridden. It was 'Apocalypse Now' but in the flesh. Over 80,000 people lost their lives in the 25 years of that conflict, including Mama's younger brother and many friends we made on several more trips there as I felt determined to support at least some locals with a trickle of tourism income. Surf travel to the Basque Country and The Canary Islands felt insignificant after that adventure. This was the taste of surfing I wanted and I kept searching for - uncrowded waves, life-changing situations, with a story to tell.

I was quickly addicted to surf exploration. 'Spots', as we call surf breaks, have personalities. It takes many swells (sometimes a lifetime) before you really appreciate their moods. And there are countless adjectives we use to describe them. Some are 'easy', pleasing to the eye, their rides fun, but not challenging. Others are 'heavy', where water can vary in weight according to the shape it takes. And the best are 'sick', and you visit them as many times as possible to 'cure' your 'disease'. But it turned out that we didn't need to travel halfway around the world to find 'sick' waves and a story to tell. Italy and the Mediterranean, right on our doorstep, offered endless possibilities that became more and more accessible as internet swell forecasting took off. Sardinia and Sicily, Puglia and Calabria, Greece and North Africa became hotspots, perfectly exposed to the swell patterns available in our enclosed basin. And they were empty of surfers.

Satellite forecasts revolutionised surf exploration in Homer's 'wine dark' Mediterranean Sea. From the days of the *Odyssey*, Mediterranean weather had been considered unpredictable and unreliable. The few surfers active before the mid 1990s had to check the beach every day in hope of a decent wave. All of a sudden the satellite swell forecasts changed that. No need to frequent smoky bars in Marina Di Ravenna to hear about what was happening out on the mussel farms. We now spent flat days behind the computer screen checking wave prediction models and exploring maps for deep water canyons, coastal bathymetry, local geology, wave fetch and calculating what effects certain low pressure systems could have on such scenarios. Big southwest depressions heading towards northwest Europe would normally activate the Mistral, a strong northwest wind that cooled above the Massif Central mountains of France, funnelling down the Rhone Valley, speeding up before it touched the Gulf of Lyon. Once it hit the Mediterranean, it sent surprisingly powerful, but short-lived (one to three days) swell south, usually between November and March. The simple rule was: where the wind hit, so did the surf. Mediterranean North Africa has good exposure to mistral swell. Day one was usually messy, day two and three cleaned up, and day four would probably be flat. So when all signs aligned, we'd explore olive groves and dirt roads, pioneering countless new breaks around the Mediterranean, and making new friends along the way, from Mafiosi to Berber fishermen.

These explorations became the realm of *SurfNews* magazine. In two years it had grown from a black and white surf club 'zine to a glossy free magazine (funded by advertising surf brands), with 10,000 copies per issue. Mazz was the photo editor (with a new 300mm Canon lens). I was the editor. It was full-time work (supplemented by my ongoing translation jobs). We had 300 square metres of office space in Ravenna, and a core member of our exploration team was Emi Cataldi from Rome. He was studying Engineering at University and had an incredible talent for surf forecasting. He cut his teeth on trips to Hawaii and Indonesia, spoke perfect English and decent Bahasa Indonesian, and was now a sponsored rider with travel budget to spend on surf trips. In 24 hours we could pull together a crack team and set off to wherever in the Mediterranean the swell was going to strike. By 2002 we had turned surf forecasting in our region into a fine art, able to determine even the hour when a swell would arrive, peak and fade.

Yet it wasn't just the science of surf forecasting that intrigued us, but the research into local culture. I was interested in any historical references to waves I could find. In one of my favourite *SurfNews* articles entitled 'Virgil's Hidden Fluctua' I had followed descriptions of barrelling waves found in Virgil's epic Latin poem *Aeneid* written between 29 and 19 BC. Using that text as a surf guide, we scored perfect pointbreaks along the Phoenician shores of North Africa. But the fine line between exploration and conquest, between exposure and exploitation, was on our mind for every trip. We could clearly see both the positive and negative effects of our endeavours in places where surfing didn't exist, and nations where it had fully developed.

In between *SurfNews* work I took a few more trips to China, and a few trips to Australia, America and around Europe, where surfing had been an industry for decades. Spots were crowded, and aggressive localism was common. I had seen what surfing could do for countries like Sri Lanka, creating small-scale wealth and job opportunities for coastal communities. The first rule of thumb was 'listen to the locals'. In one of my favourite areas of North Africa, the local crew of ten had asked us not to give away any clues in the features, not even to name the country, to avoid potential overcrowding in the future. So we started to use ancient Latin names for villages and bays, and Latin riddles, leaving the keys of future surf tourism directly in the hands of the locals - or savvy code-breakers who could decipher the clues.

CHAPTER SIX — WARTIME PERFECTION

CHAPTER SEVEN

THE SPICE ISLANDS

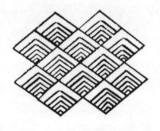

Surf exploration has a long and a colourful history, from the roots of wave-riding in Polynesia, to the intrepid Hawaiian pioneers of the early 1900s, and of course the legendary swimming Olympic gold medallist Duke Kahanamoku, who introduced modern surfing to Australia. Bruce Brown's *The Endless Summer* (1966) was the first wide appeal surf film that glorified the search for the perfect wave. Lone explorers like Peter Troy (a pioneer in Sri Lanka, and the first to surf in Italy, Argentina and Brazil) paved the way for the adventures of the likes of Kevin Naughton and Craig Petersen in the 1970s and '80s. A personal favourite in the 1990s and early 2000s was photo-explorer John Callahan. His epic images of the Philippines (naming Cloud 9 on Siargao) fuelled my travel fantasies from the pages of American published *Surfer* and *Surfing* magazines. But the more I studied the history of surf travel, the more I felt our humble Mediterranean adventures for *SurfNews* were cutting edge. We felt like we were contributing to the growing story of surf exploration.

I translated a number of our *SurfNews* articles into English and published them in *The Surfers Path,* the European alternative to the acclaimed glossy American publication *The Surfers Journal. The Surfer's Path* magazine was groundbreaking. Not only did it offer an intellectual voice for a multi-cultural surf world, it also became the first truly 'green' magazine, printed on 100 percent post-consumer recycled paper, processed without chlorine bleach with non-GMO soy inks. Under the brilliant editorship of

Caribbean raised Alex Dick-Read, a former journalist for the Associated Press, *The Surfers Path* showcased the latest work from surf science, surf art, surf culture, surf history and surf exploration. Our Mediterranean instalments from *SurfNews*, packed with hard-core adventure, laced with socio-political context, and open to discussions of sustainability and the potential negative and positive impacts of surf tourism, fitted right in. Consequently, *SurfNews* got noticed by a wider audience. John Callahan got in touch.

Callahan was now working freelance (after years as a staff photographer at *Surfer* and *Surfing*), relocated from Hawaii to Singapore, and was looking to build eclectic teams that represented surfing beyond the American, Australian and Hawaiian dominated surf pros. He was working with Brazilians, Indonesians, Japanese, South Africans, North Africans and Europeans. Callahan became intrigued by our young Mediterranean crew and started contributing stunning features to *SurfNews*. From our email exchanges, I quickly learned that Callahan was fascinated by European history, took many visits to cultural capitals of Lisbon, Paris and Rome, and was proud to see his work appealing to a growing audience of Italian surfers. Likewise, *SurfNews* readers loved his material. He had pioneered many areas in India, the Andaman and Nicobar Islands, the Philippines, Indonesia and West Africa with unrivalled research, multi-cultural travel teams, and a unique grit and determination.

In 2004 Callahan invited Emi Cataldi and I to join one of his expeditions to Indonesia, but not the usual Indian Ocean coast. "Everyone considers winter the off-season in Indonesia," read the invitation email. "We are going to prove them wrong. The goal is to explore the Maluku Islands, a remote archipelago in Pacific Indonesia." The significance was immediately clear. Since 1971 when Alby Falzon first documented perfect waves

of Bali while shooting for his sensational psychedelic film *The*
Morning of The Earth (1971), wave riders had flocked to the Bukit
peninsula. The landscape, culture and surf had constituted the
perfect backdrop for several generations of wave hungry hip-
pies. Bali offers perfect exposure to southern hemisphere winter swells in the shape of long groomed reefs, but now the island
was overloaded with surf tourists. Even the fabled Mentawai
islands off the coast of Sumatra mapped by surfers in the late
1990s had become commodified. Waves were 'sold' by the day
in luxury surf resorts or chased down to extinction by fleets of
boats, chartering wealthy crowds to the big trophies of the surf
hunt. Lance's Right and Macaroni's were the surfing equivalent
to Everest Base Camp: intense and over-crowded pieces of out-
door heaven, where foreign companies cashed in. We wanted
nothing of it.

A basic bit of research was enough to show why Maluku was
unmapped by surfers: a civil war was raging, pirates were roaming on armed speed boats, and Muslim extremists had attacked
Christian settlements (and vice versa) several times in the past
few years. But we booked our flights without blinking, and in
January landed in the tiny airport of Manado, Northern Sulawesi, found a van to take us and our surfboards, and headed for
the agreed rendezvous at Bitung harbour. The van zigzagged
through bustling markets and busy alleyways for one hour, then
pulled into the harbour under a humid sky. We paid the fee and
found the Serenade, a diving boat that Callahan had chartered
for our 21-day expedition. Its profile was far from luxurious. It
mingled perfectly with the run-down fishing fleet at berth in
the harbour. Rust stained the main deck where a local crew in
sarongs and flip flops started boarding surfboards and a few
boxes of supplies. Crewmen from other boats were looking in
disbelief at our growing load of kit. They had rarely ventured
out of the Sea of Celebes, a semi-enclosed body of water shel-

CHAPTER SEVEN – THE SPICE ISLANDS

tered from the Pacific storms, perfect for their scuba diving (hence flat water) business. But Callahan planned something completely different. He had convinced Opo, the captain, to take us to the oceanic waters of Halmahera and Morotai, the westernmost islands on the archipelago, directly exposed to North Pacific swells.

Callahan was clearly already acquainted with the crew and quietly supervised them as they brought supplies onboard from the market. He was surveying the loading procedures from atop the bow, wearing his trademark long sleeved white Lycra shirt, white hat, blue tinted polarised sunglasses, and a small satchel slung across his chest. He reached into his satchel, pulled out a packet of Marlboro, held one between his thumb and index finger, and lit up. Inhale, exhale. He looked more like a fashion photographer than an ocean roaming veteran. When he saw us on the dock he nonchalantly exhaled smoke, smiled, snapped a few shots with his bulky Canon, extinguished his cigarette, and disappeared without a word into the lower deck.

Emi and I looked at each other dubiously, boarded the boat, then mingled with the other surf travellers. They were a mix of Europeans and South Africans, all fresh from 48 hours of flying, but waiting in trepidation for the meeting Callahan had called for at "six o'clock sharp."

Callahan was raised in Honolulu, but his white skin, near ginger complexion, rounded cheek bones and icy blue eyes immediately revealed his Irish ancestry. Yet his link with Asia was strong, as with all people in Polynesia, and his wife, Jane, was Japanese. They had recently relocated from Honolulu to Singapore. It was a better base for organising freelance trips and photo shoots, mostly in Asia, then selling the content to a variety of surf and travel publications around the world. In Singapore he had also been exposed to Chinese taxi drivers, from whom he picked up the habit of growing his pinkie nail a few centimetres long, and putting it to use by unscrewing the battery box of his camera.

Callahan appeared from the lower deck just before the sun set at 5:30 pm, his satchel still slung across his chest as if permanently sown to his torso, and clearly containing all his essentials - passport, money, cell phone, compass, cigarettes, spare batteries, instant coffee sachets, candy, and who knows what else. He said nothing, but the other surfers who had travelled with him before assured me that while he is a great communicator through emails, he doesn't say that much in the flesh. 6:00 pm found us sitting in the common lounge around a bathymetry map of the Ambon District. Callahan let Sam Bleakley, European longboard champion and up-and-coming surf travel writer, welcome us. Callahan was just nodding, tickling his overgrown nail with his thumb as if to mark the passing of 'small talk'. Callahan and Sam had worked together on a number of trips before. The young and mellow Cornishman was a Cambridge University geography graduate and knew how to translate Callahan's awkward mood swings better than anyone. He was also the only one allowed access to Callahan's private cabin to consult on plans, and share a tipple of the prized bottle of rum he carried on every trip.

After all the introductions Callahan stood up, placed his fist on the desk, froze everyone with a stare, and laid the fundamental rules of the journey. "First of all, this is NOT a recreational trip. This is a MISSION. No delays will be tolerated," he said, stressing the 'not' and the 'mission' with an acute, near military tone. "We are here to work, not play." A dreadful silence followed. "Second, we don't want this area to end up like the Bukit peninsula, so please sign the coverage agreement and make sure you respect it. Fuck this up and you're out of the crew.

Finito." He planted a piercing glare onto my face. I was the only magazine editor in the group. Everyone else was a professional surfer and/or surf writer.

The agreement stated that no GPS coordinates nor evidence beyond the islands' names could be revealed in print (digital platforms were still small and social media was only just beginning). All articles had to be approved by Callahan before being published or distributed.

We all signed. Sam collected the papers, placed them in a neat folder, and handed them to Callahan, whose hands were shaking as if this apparently aggressive behaviour was merely his way to manage his own nervous nature. It soon became apparent that the seemingly arrogant style of Callahan was the way he vented frustration as a shy and generally quiet person. Above all, once he felt comfortable around you, Callahan was witty, intellectual and very quick-thinking. I got to like Callahan's quirky style from our very first conversation. He loved music, literature and history, and operated best in private discussions, not group talk (when he usually said nothing). Talking one-to-one, his glittering, deep blue eyes revealed a driven and dedicated person with an artistic and technical flair for photography and lifetime of exploration ideas as vast and ambitious as the oceans themselves.

At 11.00 pm Callahan ordered to pull anchor. "Let's rock and roll," he said from the stern, looking due west into a cloudy, starless night and performing a Mick Jagger inspired swagger as if singing 'Jumpin' Jack Flash' in his head.

As the Serenade left the harbour under intense humidity, the sweet smell of clove cigarettes smoked by the anxious crew mixed with the bitter stench of decomposing forest. This was a far cry from the harsh Bora of home I had surfed on my last session. Northeast wind had never smelled more exotic, with notes of wet grass and rancid copra fully saturating my nose.

Manado faces the northern coast of the Sulawesi Peninsula and the calm Sea of Celebes. To the south, the Sea of Maluku constitutes a water highway between the Indian and the Pacific Ocean, between Southeast Asia and Oceania. The Spice Route was the name European explorers gave to this stretch of water, starting in Achim (modern day Sumatra), touching Bantam (Java), then Sulawesi and extending west towards the 'Spice Islands' of Halmahera and Morotai. This lure of cloves and nutmeg, sold for a fortune along the smelly streets of Venice, had attracted explorers here for 500 years. The Portuguese led the way. In 1497 Vasco da Gama crossed the Cape of Good Hope and safely landed four commercial boats in Calicut, India. Then in 1511 Antònio de Abreu reached the Maluku's and another source of spices, now able to bypass Venice and the overland routes of the Silk Road. De Abreu made it to Ternate, now the capital of Halmahera, from Malacca with the help of Malay captains and a Chinese junk. His original Portuguese vessel was too clunky to handle the nearshore operations that required surgical precision (due to the local bathymetry) and was sunk by a swell in north Ambon. Those precious trade routes came at a price. The same waves we were chasing had kept the Spice Islands extremely hard to access. In his *Historia Tragico Maritima* Portugal's Bernardo Gomes de Brito (1668-1759) described several shipwrecks in these waters due to 'crazy relentless waves' breaking on coral heads 'as sharp as knives'. I had read a lot of these books when studying in Venice for the History of Exploration exam. I couldn't get de Brito's description out of my mind as we left the shelter of Talisei Island and motored east-northeast towards the turbulent mood of the winter Pacific at midnight.

The reassuring scent of landmass had now completely disappeared, replaced by the raw tang of a rising sea. The boat rocked menacingly, hit on the flanks by increasingly bigger waves. I started to count seconds between crests, as if Guancia back in Ravenna. 10, 15, then down to 5 seconds. The pulse of the swell was chaotic, coming from at least two different directions. I could not recognise any rhythm. It was just a cacophony of bigger sets, hitting at random intervals of 5 to 12 minutes.

At 2.00 am as a rainstorm pounded the deck the crew started singing. The syllabic words of Austronesian languages (Indonesian is one of them) often end in a low sounding vowel. Loud 'a's and 'o's reverberated inside the cabin, repetitive and unnerving litanies, sound-waves trapped inside a tin box. From the top bed of the bunk I was trying not to get thrown to the floor at every set wave. Even my roommate Emi, the deepest sleeper I know, was woken by the storm. It was a long and restless night.

The storm eased just before dawn. Captain Opo had heavy dark rings under his eyes and fire red pupils at sunrise. The crew must have smoked one hundred cigarettes and sang as many animistic songs, meant to calm the raging waters.

We ate, read, ate, traded stories with the crew, cracked jokes with Callahan, and later that day we had the first and dramatic sight of northern Halmahera. In an immaculate blue sky, the Dukono, a huge active volcano, revealed white ash rising up to the troposphere, then bent westwards by the ocean breeze. Black basalt and whitewater appeared to be the *yin* and *yang* of this coastline, akin to Haiti and parts of Hawaii, where tall mountains, lush thick valleys and deep bays dominated the shore. We motored past waterfalls cascading down 20 metre cliffs directly into the ocean. There was a solid six feet swell, the saltwater whipped to a white froth by the wind. But the bays were too deep, and we couldn't find any surfable breaks. Instead we saw manta rays, dolphins and bought fresh fish from locals, operating in small Polynesian-style outrigger canoes. Their boats looked like a natural extension of their limbs, handling hooks, nets, fish, money, then paddling away for another catch.

Emi's GPS allowed us to infer our precise latitude and longitude, but electronic bathymetry maps of the area had been restricted by the Indonesian army. So we were dependent on a trusted Royal Admiralty map dated 1920, with water depth measured in fathoms (one fathom equals 1.8 m). We took turns inspecting the starboard side for obstacles, and found the first rideable wave almost unintentionally, late in the afternoon, checking the sheltered corner of a vast bay for a safe anchorage to spend the night.

Emi was the first out, jumping off deck with his board before the Serenade had even anchored. The waves were mediocre, but in the dead of European winter, with Italy in the firm grasp of freezing Bora, these tropical shoulders looked like pure gold. "All clear," shouted Emi. "Nice and deep, and no rocks," he added, hair still dry after a long ride. We soon joined him in the line-up. Head high left-handers were refracting on a shallow reef ledge. A punchy take off was followed by a peeling shoulder that ran all the way to the beach, exhaling its last breath at the foot of a Christian village of a few hundred inhabitants named Sopi. We surfed until dark and paddled out the following morning. All of a sudden, five local teenage boys wearing tight sarongs and carrying wooden planks crossed the crammed strip of sand and entered the water. They paddled out in no time, exchanged smiles, but quickly focused on catching waves. As the next set appeared, three of them spun their finless boards and took the drop on the same wave, riding prone, bumping into each other, but still holding a precise line.

"Those are *paipos*," noted Callahan, who was launching the zodiac to shoot the surf session from a closer angle. *Paipo* means 'short' in Hawaiian. These thin belly boards, 4 to 6 feet in length, constitute the original Polynesian wave craft. Use of *paipos*, especially among kids, has been documented around the Pacific and Atlantic for at least 1,000 years. Callahan had seen them in action from Madagascar to São Tomé. But these kids were not simply playing on crude equipment. They were riding with a fast and effective technique, propelling with arms and legs (no flippers) to produce great bursts of speed on what looked like specially designed equipment. One of them, the oldest, took off behind the boil, charged high up the steep face, and released the leading rail causing the *paipo* to slide backwards, spinning a full 180 degrees. By now he was connecting to the second section, catapulting down the line, but going backwards and looking back into the barrel behind him, and in complete control, finally sliding the *paipo* around to complete the full 360. As the wave faded out, he somehow sustained forward thrust and connected to the inside section, riding all the way to the beach. "Did you guys see that?" I screamed, amazed by this radical manoeuvre. "That's the coolest 360 I've ever seen," added Emi, equally amazed.

His ride had been the longest ridden all morning and the villagers welcomed it with hoots and whistles from the beach. But what blew me away was the positioning of his board. I had never seen a board in that part of the wave before. It used as much below the water as upon and above, akin to the dynamic of a dolphin, rising in and out of the face. For surfers grown up in the post George Greenough era - Greenough invented the modern fin and inspired the shortboard revolution in the mid to late 1960s by showcasing on his knees what could be done standing up - sliding, as these kids were doing, down the face of a wave sideways was more often seen as a sign of board malfunction than a controlled line. 'Good' surfing was defined by 'controlled turns' and rarely by slides. The contrast in approaches with our crew of foreign riders on conventional short and longboards was striking. Our crew were performing vertical manoeuvres, matching the wave power with torque and compression. They knifed deep bottom turns, threw critical top-turns, and released fans of whitewater while cutting back, all aided by their three finned 'thrusters'.

The local kids, in contrast, left practically no wake. Their finless boards travelled flat, frictionless, gliding effortlessly between pockets of wave power. Their skills were all about sliding and keeping momentum, not about carving and stalling. They were doing what Hawaiians call *lala*. In the tradition of *lala*, sliding, then regaining composure on the wave face, was an integral part of Polynesian surfing. *Lala* is a sign of controlled abandon, a deliberate choice where the rider voluntarily refuses to steer, releasing the rail, and allowing the wave to take over. *Lala* requires a large amount of muscular control, from the core and thighs, to keep the board slotted in the wave as it slips away from the rider all the time. Speed is essential to prevent losing control.

In contrast, modern shortboard surfing is far more about staying in trim, high or low on the wave face, where balance is essential, dictated as much from the top half of the body as the lower half. Cheyne Cottrell, one of the South African riders on the trip, and easily the most talented shortboarder in the crew, was so inspired that he followed the local line and threw a long 'carving' (not 'sliding') 360 on the same section. The beach exploded. Emi was equally inspired, and traded boards with one of the kids, riding like a champion as he controlled three perfect 360s on one wave. Meanwhile, the kid who borrowed Emi's board was eager to switch back, apparently not interested in the modern equipment.

We continued to share waves, then took the zodiac ashore to meet the village. We went to register our arrival, passports in hand, escorted by 50 smiling kids and a few of the local surfers and their parents. We soon got to know their story from the village head. The language spoken here was Ternate Malay, also Malay-Austronesian in heritage. But some of the crew could translate into Bahasa, and Emi (fluent in Bahasa) could then tell us in English. They knew the Bahasa word for 'surfing' - *selancar* - which they had been doing prone on wooden boards for tens of generations. But they called it *lao maeng* 'sea play'. They had seen some travelling 'modern surfers' way back in 1983 when an Australian yacht took shelter in the bay and visited the village for a few days. The captain surfed with the locals and left a board with them. 21 years later the board had fallen apart, and the kids preferred to use their traditional equipment anyway, shaped from locally sourced hard wood. The problem with the gift was as soon as it got damaged they didn't have any fibreglass to fix it.

We were taken to the so-called 'canoe shop'. A slim man in his 40s, with sun-bleached fuzzy hair and teeth stained red from chewing the stimulant betel-nut, greeted us enthusiastically. His front yard was filled with outrigger canoes being repaired. The small canoes, used for near shore fishing or trade, were carved out of a single sturdy log, carefully selected and felled in the nearby mountains. They are light and lively, thanks to one, or more commonly two outriggers, fastened to the main hull with cords made of bark and plant and tree fibres. There were no pins or metal parts. A few bigger canoes were six to eight metres long and could carry up to 15 people, designed for longer distance travel.

The man at the 'canoe shop' was the shaper for all the *paipos*. He showed us his tools - simple iron axes and volcanic stones for sanding. He had two *paipo* models, both cut from a single slab of dark oily hard wood. The 'big wave' model sported a straight outline, a beaky nose and a perpendicular handle for extra grip (a feature not used on Hawaiian *paipos*). The 'small wave' model was wider, flatter and was easier to manoeuvre thanks to a hip 30 cm from the tail.

On our final morning in Sopi we had one last surf with the locals, pulled anchor and left. We had a few hundred miles of coast to map on the way to Morotai, the westernmost and most promising island of the Maluku archipelago. We found exceptional untapped surf in the two weeks that followed and surfed our brains out. But the sessions at Sopi were the highlight for me, and after this trip I started to think very differently about the conventional history of surfing. Clearly wave-riding could evolve naturally in a wide variety of wave environments and become an integral part of the cultural fabric of a place. I was hungry to learn more.

98

CHAPTER EIGHT

A NEW BEGINNING

Back in Ravenna I continued to edit *SurfNews* with a new-found interest into the rich history of surfing. In Sopi, the links with Polynesia seemed obvious, and the disregard for the surfboard left in the 1980s had made this community even more fascinating, perhaps inspiring a few modern lines, but reinforcing a love of traditional equipment that exists in wave-riding communities all over Papua and the Pacific. And of course, the links to Polynesia extended further than the *paipos*. The small dugout canoes, drying their hulls in the sun, waiting to be repaired, were quintessentially Polynesian. Seafaring Malay-Austronesians (the ancestors of Polynesians) historically used this efficient boat in their trade routes. And these trade routes started approximately 2000 years BC in southern China, connecting a big triangle from the Yangtze delta, Taiwan to the east, and Hainan island to the south. Thanks to accurate navigation techniques using stars, bird observation and detailed knowledge of waves, swells and weather patterns, these ocean-roaming people from modern-day China slowly migrated on dugout canoes into an area of ocean that stretches from the Philippines, through Indonesia and New Zealand, Tahiti, Hawaii, to Easter Island in the South Pacific and Madagascar in the Indian Ocean.

In *A History of Early Southeast Asia* Kenneth Hall describes Austronesians as 'nomads of the southern oceans' and compares these early mariners to the gypsies of the northern steppe in their expert roles of trading, settling and exploring. Austronesian sailors were documented in China from the 3rd century BC during the Han dynasty (206 BC - 220 AD). Even Roman historian Pliny the Elder (who died during the eruption of Pompeii in 79 BC) noted in *Natural History* the Austronesians intimate knowledge of the oceans, reporting how their double-hulled 'rafts' were 'neither steered by rudder nor drawn or impelled by oars or sails. (Instead) they chose the winter season for their voyage, for then a wind is blowing, guiding them in a straight course from gulf to gulf.'

It turns out that some of the oldest dugout canoes, from 8,000 years ago, have been found where ancient river and coastal cultures developed in Africa and Asia. The Dufuna canoe has been excavated in modern day Nigeria, West Africa, while the Kuahuqiao canoe was found in Zhejiang province, China, where the Qiantang River flows into Hangzhou Bay. The early Neolithic Kuahuqiao culture flourished in the region which became an important population centre occupied by the Hemudu and Majiabang cultures by 5000 BC. By 3000 BC these cultures had evolved into the Liangzhu civilization, genetically linked to modern Austronesian people today.

When English explorer Captain James Cook and the crews aboard the *Resolution* and *Discovery* met Polynesians at the end of the 18th century, they described fleets of 300 canoes, some over 30 metres in length and carrying up to 300 passengers. But most of them were small pirogues, just like the ones in Sopi, Halmahera. Flexible and strong, equipped with a triangular sail, they were (and still are) a perfect device for near shore fishing and small commerce. And they can glide on waves as well. Could wave riding, as witnessed in Sopi, be a by-product of the Austronesian diaspora? It is very likely that knowledge was exchanged between areas. These sea faring cultures had no written language, no wheel and no iron tools, but their water skills have been unprecedented.

However, it is not easy to determine exactly when and how early forms of wave riding spread. And quite frankly, wave riding doesn't even need a link with Polynesia to evolve. Observing nature alone - such as sea birds and sea creatures saving precious energy by moving with waves and tides - offers a model for wave-riding. And using waves to propel a craft in water is an essential skill if you live on the coast and need to go in and out of a bay with your fishing equipment. This can be dangerous work, so transforming the danger of the surf into a safe place to play is an important practice to pass on fishing traditions to kids. Fishing communities from South America, West Africa to South Asia to Southern Europe have been playing in the waves for centuries, and teaching their kids about sea-life, rip currents and tides. And those kids in turn would pass on the tradition, and no doubt continue to enjoy themselves in the surf.

Traces of 'functional' wave riding on reed-canoes are documented in Peru from 1000 BC with the fabled *Caballitos de Totora*, and Peru continues to have a thriving surf culture today. The pounding surf of West Africa no doubt inspired ancient canoe cultures to ride waves, but without a written language, we have to await the first European accounts from the 1500 and 1600s that describe the incredible swimming ability of the coastal communities and their wave-riding antics in canoes. Surf historians, such as Ben Finney and Matt Warshaw, agree that Polynesian wave-riding was developed as Austronesian migration reached places like Tonga, Samoa, The Easter Islands, Fiji and even Maluku. But in most places, it was a kids pastime. However, on the islands of eastern Polynesia - Hawaii, Marquesas, Tahiti, Cook Islands and New Zealand - wave-riding was also practiced by adults. When Tahitians settled in Hawaii in around 1000 AD, wave-riding developed into a complex cultural practice known as *he'e nalu* ('wave-sliding') with advanced riding techniques (such as *lala*), dedicated competitions, deities and specific board design.

Polynesians had no written language, therefore their cultural heritage, often revolving around waves and transoceanic voyages, was left to stories, songs, pictographs and tattoos. The earliest literary traces of Polynesian wave-riding are recorded in Tahiti and Hawaii by Europeans between 1769 and 1779, the most recited credited to Lieutenant James King who took Captain James Cook's place in compiling the Pacific voyage journals after Cook's death. King was amazed by this 'diversion' performed by the locals in breaking waves, but didn't try to give it a name. And it's this Hawaiian version of wave-riding that pollinated western culture in the beginning of the 20th century, creating what we now call 'surfing'.

Surf writer Daniel Duane explained that the word 'surf' entered the English vocabulary in 1685 and was likely an alteration of a Sanskrit word '*suffe*' meaning 'coastline' familiar to Portuguese traders along the coast of India. But for centuries 'surf' only indicated the area where waves broke, not the act of riding them.

While it is widely agreed that Polynesians stood riding boards, the first European illustration of a stand-up rider is actually on the Kerala coast of India, researched by Australian surf historian Geoff Cater. Englishman Charles Gold, who served with the Royal Artillery on India's southern coast, sketched 'Madrassan Men Surfing' at the end of the 18th century. His illustration was published in 1806 in London. It depicts a man standing on a board made of fastened logs being propelled by a breaking wave, holding a plank of wood in his hands and a feathered turban on his head. Geoff Cater discusses the different environments, comparing the abundant buoyant timber available in Hawaii to make solid surfboards, to the rice growing plains in Kerala that might have inspired fisherman to lash together separate logs to make a buoyant surf craft. Interestingly the Madrassan surfer is utilising a parallel stance, very similar to the one used by Polynesian riders depicted in western sketches throughout the 19th century. This posture, also called 'penguin stance', is the precursor of the modern-day 'sideways stance' where feet are placed perpendicular to the board, one in front of the other. Even if parallel stance is stable enough to guarantee long rides on small waves, it does not allow any of the manoeuvres performed today. The rider is heading almost straight towards the beach, and the board the Madrassan is using doesn't look as refined as the first illustration of a surfboard credited to John Webber, who in 1779 portrayed riders in Kealakekua Bay, Hawaii. The Madrassan boards, made of long round logs, would have lacked the speed and control of the flat, more hydrodynamic Polynesian designs, that used glide, flexibility and sharp biting rails.

It was in this context of passionately reading about the history of surfing that I took a lone surf trip through southeastern China before travelling inland and unexpectedly coming across the Temple of surfing Buddhas in Yunnan.

The surfing *luohan*s carved in the 1880s are utilising a contemporary stance, cutting sideways, along the unbroken face of the wave, riding on fishes and other mythological animals.

After speaking to the Abbot, I caught the bus back to Kunming. It was crammed with rowdy tourists from the Northeast, smoking and playing cards. Even among this cacophony my mind couldn't stop processing what I had just stumbled on, and the mysterious words of the Abbot, with *nong chao er* written in grass style cursive in my moleskin notebook. The next morning I went straight to the main art gallery in Kunming. I found out that there are eight temples in China showcasing a '500 *luohan*' installation, but none of them on the coast. They are all land-locked and randomly scattered all over the country from Beijing (the Jade Cloud Temple) in the north to Chengdu (the Baoguan Temple) in the southwest. In 2001 the Central Art Committee declared this art-form worth protecting. Each one of the 4,000 statues was photographed and catalogued. But only the *luohan* of the Qiongzhu Temple are catching waves. What makes it even stranger is that the artist Li Guangxiu had been commissioned to do a similar decoration for the Baoguan Temple in his home-town Chengdu (Sichuan province), just three years prior to working on the Qiongzhu Temple. But no waves and no surfers can be found in there.

From Yunnan I travelled to Lhasa, eventually reaching the Rongbuk monastery, the highest in the world at 4,980 metres just under the Mount Everest Base Camp in Tibet. From there I slowly worked my way back east into the agricultural heart of China to Yangshuo and the rice terraces of Longji. Trekking through bamboo groves and karst peaks of Longji was unforgettable. These were once again the landscapes portrayed in *Journey to the West* that I longed to experience. And staying with a Zhuang minority family in a village in the mountains will live with me forever. But of course I could not get the surfing Buddhas out of my mind, and when I finally made it to the coast, I had a few days in Hong Kong before I flew out of China. The only surf depiction I could find there was a temple built in the 1960s with a bronze statue of a monk riding a stylised wave on a carp decorated by a Yunnanese team of artists, surely directly inspired by the Qiongzhu Temple in their home region. Then in Tai Long Wan (otherwise known as Big Wave Bay), in southern Hong Kong, I scored a fantastic swell with the community of expats and handful of Chinese surfers riding waves in a sub-tropical Eden just a short distance from the overwhelming skyscrapers of one the world's most bustling economic and cultural centres. I was loath to leave, but had commitments at *Surf-News* magazine.

Back home in Italy my research continued. Could European descriptions of Polynesian, African or Indian wave-riding have inspired Li Guangxiu? Or was this wave in Kunming telling a whole different story? How could the artist so realistically depict surfers, and wave-riding biomechanics if he had not seen any? How can a riverside town like Hangzhou, the capital of modern Zhejiang province, and the place the Abbot suggested I should go to, be related to surfing, or to any form of wave-riding?

The first thing I considered was the receptivity of foreign cultural practices inside the Chinese community at the time when Li Guangxiu was active. Sino-European relations were actually at their lowest during the late 19th century. The British East India Company wanted to buy vast quantities of tea from China, but China was self-sufficient, so once the ruling class had a good amount of Spanish silver from the Americas for their tea, they didn't need anything else. To get the upper hand in the trade relationship, the British devised a terrible plan. They could sell textiles (made with Indian cotton) for Indian grown opium, and then flood the Chinese market until there was a demand for the drug. A full generation of young Chinese, mainly from coastal towns, suffered from chronic drug addiction.

Western powers were giving a terrible example of global trade. Foreigners drained the economy and lowered the esteem of the people for the ruling Qing dynasty, triggering xenophobic sentiments. In a letter to Queen Victoria in 1839 Commissioner Lin pleaded the British to have a conscience and stop destroying the nation with opium. But Confucian morals had little say in a new era of global greed and maritime super powers.

The subsequent two Opium Wars (1839-1842 and 1856-1860) over British trade in China seriously disrupted the nation, weakening the Qing dynasty and forcing new trade routes to open with the wider world. In the Treaty of Nanjing that ended the first Opium War, Hong Kong was ceded to the British, and other strategic ports favoured European trade, the deals imposed on China by means of cannons, more Indian opium, and the ocean vessels of Queen Victoria.

By the peace treaty of the second Opium War, 80 ports were established in China with favourable trade terms to foreign powers. Around 30 million lost their lives, mainly because of famine, during those years. In these desperate times, many Chinese were encouraged to move abroad. The first contingent of 500 Chinese workers arrived in California in 1850, employed mainly in gold mines. They came from the coastal towns of Fujian and Guangdong and called themselves 'coolies', a term derived from 苦力 *kǔlì* meaning 'bitter work'. They had signed contracts based on false promises. Others had sold themselves to pay for gambling and opium related debts. The working conditions they were willing to accept were horrifying. Their wages were half the amount that regular workers would expect.

In 1862 when US President Abraham Lincoln signed the Railroad Act to link east and west coasts with railroad and telegraph, the number of cheap Chinese labourers soared exponentially. News of 'coolies' being beaten to death and hanged at the railway poles in Los Angeles, California, was reaching the state-controlled media of dynastic China just when Li Guangxiu was working on the Qiongzhu Temple in Yunnan. I therefore doubt that wave-riding reported in English by white colonial explorers would have inspired a state sponsored artist in rural China.

Ironically, the same railroad largely built by desperate Chinese labourers would bring middle class white investors to California's first 'surfing exhibition' in 1907. Raised in Hawaii

with Irish ancestry, surfer George Freeth was advertised on bill-
boards as 'the Hawaiian wonder who could walk on water', and
was hired by the Pacific Electric railroad to entertain audiences
twice a week, riding a huge finless wooden board beside the Re-
dondo pier. The company hoped to lure the public into making
regular trips to the Pacific in its railways carriages. Hawaii, now
annexed territory of the US, was also a new tourist destination
where surfing was marketed as a healthy, exhilarating activity.
In California, as commercial sunscreens were manufactured and
tanning became socially accepted, surfing represented the out-
door lifestyle and liberal values developers wanted to showcase
and promote to attract people to the coast.

Ironically this was all built on both the appropriation of an
ancient Polynesian culture, once heavily suppressed by European colonising missionaries, and the railroad industry, built
with cheap Chinese labour, expropriating the land of Native
Americans.

Relations between China and the English colonial coastlines
of India, home of those 'Madrassan Men Surfing', were equally
poor when Li Guangxiu was working on the Qiongzhu Temple.
Indians were extensively deployed against China in the Opium
Wars, assigned as a security force in the colonial concessions of
Shanghai and Amoy. The Chinese even had a derogatory word
for the Indian troops who wore characteristic red turbans - 紅頭
阿三 hóngtóu ā sān 'red-headed servants'. Out of this global humiliation - a period the Chinese call 'the Century of Shame' - a
hatred for outsiders rose, paving the way for national resistance,
Communism, and ultimately Maoism.

It is also unlikely that West African canoe surfing or even ancient Peruvian wave-riding would have influenced Li Guangxiu. Clearly the annals of surf history and global socio-political

relationships were a dead end to understand the *luohan* of the Qiongzhu Temple sharing waves. Those translation geeks back at University in Venice were my role models here. My next surf trip was not going to be inspired by a dot to explore on a map, but words to explore in the dictionaries. I needed to do philological research into China's 5,000 years of dynastic culture on those words 弄潮兒 *nong chao er*. I wiped the dust off *The Mathews* dictionary, picked up my University texts, and planned the first visit in over a decade to Ca' Foscari's library in Venice.

CHAPTER EIGHT — A NEW BEGINNING

CHAPTER NINE

RIVERS AND REVOLUTIONS

I picked a flat day to take the train ride from Ravenna to Venice. The sky was locked under a cold high-pressure spell. It was still, windless and cursed with low white clouds. Mariners call this 'bonaccia', a sarcastic take on the Latin word bonum (good). Ravenna and Venice do not see the sun for weeks when enveloped in Bonaccia. While the surf producing wind patterns of the Bora, Scirocco, Mistral and Libeccio are the boat crushing yang terrifying mariners for 5,000 years, Bonaccia is the yin stillness, marked by continental high pressure, and freezing temperatures for thousands of kilometres from Ravenna to eastern Russia.

Just north of Ferrara, the train crossed the Po plain into Veneto, passing reed flanked marshes and dark, freshly ploughed beetroot farms. The Po river, at its driest in winter, barely occupies a fraction of its summer bed, leaving vast swathes of shallow ponds, the realm of lugubrious grey herons and restless wintertime mosquitoes. Under Bonaccia, the fog dominates. It creeps over the mud and coats the entire landscape in layers of oppressive vaporised alabaster.

The Po, known quite simply to locals as 'Il Fiume' (The River), is Italy's biggest river. It marks the boundary between the continental and subtropical weather zones. To the south is the quintessential sun-baked Mediterranean landscape of hills, olive groves and vineyards. To the north it becomes a flat expanse, criss-crossed by dykes, old farmhouses and doomed to long cold winters.

The train sped past battalions of poplars. Their trunks were surrounded by thorny brambles, as if trapped at the western end of the Silk Road, unable to proceed. They were emblems for the merciless winter here. It triggers heavy symptoms of 'eastern anxiety' for those who cannot afford to leave. It's a claustrophobic sense of immobility that can only be cured with a departure, or a storm. Ferrara's poet Lodovico Ariosto (1474-1533) wrote about the effects of this weather-induced depression on Adriatic people in his epic romance *Orlando Furioso*: '(They) loath the lazy calm's repose, and pray that stormy waves may lash the beach.'

Adriatic surfers can go mad during Bonaccia. Lodovico 'Guancia' Baroncelli used to tell me about an infamous winter before I started surfing when a Bonaccia lasted 75 days. "By the time the first swell hit Ravenna in March," he said, "we'd lost a few million neurones to LSD and amphetamines. Some surfers had sold their cars and fled abroad, others were busted for selling drugs and sent to jail."

Today's trip to Venice felt like a way to show that Bonaccia wouldn't get the better of me. The train pulled into the station, but the whole city was caked in mist. As I crossed the Grand Canal, only The Bridge of the Barefoot Monks came into view. Everything else - boats, souvenir shops, people - had been enveloped in thick fog. People emerged from the brume at the last moment, like ghosts coming and going, as ephemeral as waves.

Under this kind of visual blanket Venice's intimate smells strike the hardest: the wet stone of old walls, the sugar of freshly baked 'cats' tongues' biscuits, the low-tide stench of rotting seaweed, and most overwhelming of all, sewage. These smells crept around the city, got cornered at the feet of high walls and trapped under terraces. I literally got intoxicated by these smells as I walked around. I 'became' Venice again.

Of course, I got lost. Thirteen years had passed since studying here. The Chinese department had moved out of Campo San Polo and it took me over one hour to locate Ca' Foscari's central library in the western district of Dorsoduro. But once I found it, the re-assuring smell of dust rising from heavy-bound books made me feel at home.

Translating the three characters given by the Abbot had al-ready started in *The Mathews*. 弄 *Nong* is 'playing' or 'fooling with'. 潮 *Chao* is 'tide'. 兒 *Er* is 'children'. A simple translation is therefore 'children of the tide' or 'children fooling with the tide' or 'fooling with the tide' or 'playing with the tide'. But where are the waves? Who are the 'children of the tide'? And what are they riding? This is why I came to Ca' Foscari.

The starting point was a dictionary of Chinese etymology. The librarian delivered it to my desk with a thump. Dust scat-tered from the worn blue cover and I sneezed. I tackled the index as if looking for the fabled X on a treasure map. This particular dictionary analysed 1,000 individual characters, extending as far back as the first recorded form, then documenting their evolu-tion and usage to modern times. Most words used today can be traced back to a style called 甲骨文 *jiǎ gǔ wén* ('language of shells and bones') commonly known as 'oracle bone script', from the Shang dynasty that flourished in the valley of the Yangtze River from the 16th to the 11th century BC. Shang dynasty kings wore silk robes and managed vast armies, utilising bronze weapons and horse chariots.

This form of divination was used any time the King of the Shang wanted to connect to the spirits of his ancestors. Questions ranging from warfare to weather were carved on flat bones using a bronze pin. Oxen scapulae or turtle plas-trons were then charred until the organic matter cracked open. Divinations were deduced by reading the patterns of such breaches. The 'answers' were then carved on the same bones. These 'oracular bones' give us the deepest shamanic meaning of Chinese characters, and are directly linked to modern Chinese.

All of the three characters in *nong chao er* are reported in *jia gu wen*. The first translation of 弄 *nong* is 'to manipulate'. Its oldest form revolves around the component 'jade', possibly a precious bowl, in the middle 玉, surrounded by two stylised hands holding it. Over time *nong* has come to mean 'playing a musical instrument', but also 'toying with', 'fooling with' or 'activating', and even 'deceiving'.

Chao's 潮 first translation is 'tide', the alternate rising and falling of the sea level caused by the gravity of the moon and sun. Chinese dictionaries often couple this with 'river bore' and use the word 'wave' as one of the possible translations. This is a vital clue, leading inland. I took a deep breath, and went on translating.

The dictionary explained every graphic component of *chao*. On the left we have the radical for water 氵 also defined as 'wet' and 'damp'. On the top and bottom of the central part we can see the components 'grass' enclosing a 'sun' 日 *ri*. The right part 月 *yuè* stands for 'moon' and suggests the periodicity of the phenomenon. Patch all this together, and the description reads, 'in the morning the sun rises, casting light on the meadows along the river banks, and the water level periodically rises'.

潮, *chao*
Tide
Oracle bone script

The use of the word 'tide' is strictly dependent on the context. If you take away the radical for water 氵 on the left, for example, 'tide' turns into 朝 *cháo* 'imperial court' or 'dynasty'. It was a prerogative of dynastic kings of the Shang to perform rites at sunrise, to guarantee peace and prosperity to the fields and rivers. This form of 'tide' can also be pronounced '*zhāo*', meaning 'day', 'dawn' or 'period of time'.

Further, if you add 'tide' with a particular adjective, for example 'public' (工 *gōng*), you have 'insurrection' or 'unrest'. Several western sinologists, notably Karl August Wittfogel (1896-1988), referred to the Chinese empire as a 'hydraulic oligarchy'. Yu the Great (2200-2100 BC) was known as the 'Great Tamer of Floods' for introducing flood control and inaugurating dynastic rule in China by establishing the Xia dynasty (2070-1600 BC).In 1046 BC the Shang dynasty was overthrown at the Battle of Muye, and the Zhou dynasty (until 256 BC) was established, who set out the 'mandate of heaven' to claim that there could be only one legitimate ruler of China at a time, and that this ruler had the blessing of the gods.

But real control of the country came from controlling the waterways (that were often read as being controlled by the gods). Failing to do so would trigger floods and famines able to topple even the most advanced dynasty. The reason is strictly climatic: the dry continental weather of northern and central China would not allow diffused agriculture, so a strong despotic set of institutions were required to build and maintain a vast, centralised, irrigation system. Throughout Chinese history, social turmoil has correlated with the mismanagement of waterways and estuaries. And consequently, uprising and revolution has spread along these waterways. Certainly, rivers offer great symbols for Chinese history. A Chinese proverb says, 'history is a mirror' and the quasi periodic flooding of rivers are a metaphor for cycles of order and disorder in Chinese politics. But people have some-

In the 1340s China's second largest river, the Yellow River, flooded constantly, causing uprisings that would ultimately topple the powerful Mongolian Yuan dynasty (1259-1368). Secret societies such as the White Lotus constituted a major threat for the ruling class in times of distress. They fused elements of Buddhism, Manichaeism and local shamanic beliefs. Their followers also envisioned the downfall of corrupt leaders, and the return of Maytreya, the oncoming Buddha, bringing forth abundance and stability. The Red Turban Rebellion (named after the use of distinguishing red banners and red turbans) between 1351 and 1368 gathered momentum along the main waterways of central and northern China, fiercely fighting the unjust regency along China's two biggest rivers, the Yangtze and the Yellow River, and even capturing Pyongyang (in North Korea) from their base on the Yalu River. A raging tide of angry peasants and waterway workers toppled the Mongolian Yuan and gave birth to the glorious Ming dynasty (1368-1644). I was now starting to wonder if the *Luohan* of the Qiongzhu Temple were some kind of surfing revolutionaries.

The colour red is a constant presence throughout these revolutions and rivers in China, but red has always been a hugely important colour in Chinese culture. As early as the Shang dynasty the colour was believed to possess a spiritual power of fire, sun and vitality that repelled demons, and so was applied to doors and the exteriors of buildings as a barrier. The red pigment was originally extracted from the mineral cinnabar - a cranberry-hued ore - through labour intensive mining in Guizhou and Hunan provinces in the south. The difficulties in sourcing the colour made it even more highly desirable. And the mining process had a deadly side, the ore laced with poisonous mercury. Over time red grew to stand for happiness, good fortune and protection - and the go to colour for any important occasion, from festival to revolution. When the Chinese Communist party adopted the red of Moscow in the former Soviet Union, the colour already had deep lure throughout Chinese society. A famous person is *hong le*, or simply 'red'. If you're jealous, then you're 'red-eyed' of the *hong huo* or 'red fire' lifestyle they lead - meaning their life burns bright and ever more vigorous, like a blazing bonfire. *Chengyu* such as this - concise, elegant idioms and proverbs - pepper the Chinese language. According to one classic example, 'red ink stains red, black ink black' which means 'you're judged by the company you keep'. For the Chinese, red ink is good.

Going back to the definition of *chao*, 'tide' can also convey love and emotion. The word 'high tide' 高潮 *gāo cháo*, for example, is translatable with 'orgasm' in modern Chinese. This sexual implication of 'tide' is traced in literature back to the 1st century. *The Spring and Autumn Apocrypha* (春秋纬), a commentary compiled during the Western Han Dynasty (206BC-25AD), stated that 'young women are as strong as the river tide' (牛女為江潮 *niúnǔ wéi jiāng cháo*). Further, tide can mean 'fashionable', 'trendy' or 'edgy' in expressions such as 'currents of thought' (思潮 *sī cháo*), 'new wave' (新潮 *xīn cháo*) and 'emotional uplift' (心潮 *xīn cháo*).

The English use of 'tide' derives from the Proto-Germanic '*tidiz*' and shares the same etymology as '*zeit*' (time). Religious words such as '*shrovetide*' (Shrove Tuesday and the two days preceding it when it was advisable to take confession) and '*whitsuntide*' (the weekend) still bear traces of this origin. 'Tide' came to mean the rising and falling of the ocean in the late Middle Ages, alongside 'ebb' and 'flood', derived from old Frisian, a Germanic language spoken on the shores of the North Sea. In Latin languages, tide is '*mare*' ('*marèe*' in French and '*marea*' in Spanish and Italian), indicating a clear connection to 'the sea'. But in Chinese, 潮 *cháo* has more reference to 'river' (河 *hé* or 江 *jiāng*) than 'sea' (海 *hǎi*). So how can 'tide' be so prevalent in the rivers of mainland China?

China is bisected by tens of great rivers, creating the fertile lowlands that have nurtured Chinese civilisation. Several of these rivers, from the Pearl River in the southern subtropical area of Guangdong, to the Yellow River in the colder Shandong province in the north, have 'river bores', 'river tides', 'tidal waves' or 'tidal bores'. A tidal bore can happen twice a day on incoming tides when water flows upstream, rather than downstream, but will be most prevalent around spring tides, during new and full moons. The tidal phenomenon is biggest in the Spring and Autumn equinoxes when the moon and sun fall into alignment with the Earth, and their gravitational pull is strongest, causing river bores to travel upstream at great speeds, for great distances and form an audible noise.

China's river bores are driven by the extreme tidal range of the East China Sea. This is nine metres during the Spring and Autumn equinoxes, triggering huge movements of water. Couple this with the vast estuaries of major rivers such the Qiantang and the Yangtze, and during incoming tides, water is funnelled up river for hundreds of kilometres, twice a day. This notion of bi-diurnal tides is testified in the character 汐 *xī*, formed by 'water' and 'dusk', meaning the 'nighttime' - as opposed to 'daytime' - tide, and inevitably there is a long history of Chinese art, science and writing on river bores.

The first appearance of a 'tidal wave' in Chinese literature is in the *History of the Southern States of Wu and Yue* compiled by Han dynasty (206 BC - 220 AD) historian Zhao Ye. Emperor Fu Chai condemned Minister Wu Zixu to death (in 484 BC) because he didn't trust his military advice, ordering him to be boiled alive in a cauldron, sown inside a leather sack and thrown into the river, close to modern day Hangzhou (where the Abbot said I might find out more about the *nong chao er*). But Wu Zixu's infuriated soul 'enraged the waters' until they 'rose in great billows causing havoc among his enemies'. This was of course a river bore of the Qiantang River 錢塘江 or Qiántáng jiāng (as 'jiang' also means 'river'). The shape of the river itself is compared to the Chinese character 之 *zhī*, leading to the name the Zhe (bent) River, or 折江 *Zhéjiāng*. Consequently, the 'bent river' gives the province of Zhejiang its name, with Hangzhou as its capital. The 'Z (or S) bend' was perfect for creating a spectacular river bore wave up to five metres high and travelling at an average of 15 km per hour.

The first scientific description of the river bore phenomenon, described as the 'tide-head' (潮頭 *cháo tóu*), also appears in the Han dynasty and is also on the Qiantang. Philosopher Wang Chong (27-100 AD) linked the 'tide-head' with lunar phases in his essay *Lunheng*: 'the Three Rivers, upon entering the ocean, begin to roar and foam in their channels, which are usually narrow and shallow and thus rise as great waves. The rising of waves follows the growing and waning, the fullness and extinction of the moon'.

Chinese scientists accurately predicted tide cycles much earlier than their western counterparts. The first tidal measurement happened during the Tang dynasty (618-907) in 770 BC when Dou Shumeng came up with figures less than one second different from modern calculations. Dou Shumeng was from Zhejiang province, where he witnessed the river bore climbing inland along the banks of the Qiantang. The first published tide tables are on the Qiantang in 1056. In contrast, the first recorded tide chart in the West appeared in London in 1213, developed for the convenience of shipping. China, meanwhile, was also interested in the spectacle of the river bore. In Hangzhou, the tidal bore pattern has been celebrated for thousands of years.

But what about the last word in *nong chao er*? 兒 *Ér* stands for 'children' or 'young person'. The original character resembles a newly born baby. In the upper part you can see the cranial bones still open and not fully formed, while the bottom part is constituted of the pictogram 'person' 人 *rén*. This infers that 'river-side child', 'river-side girl' or 'river-side boy' could also be a translation of *nong chao er*.

Around noon I took a break, ate some lunch, and returned refreshed, leafing through my translation notes. *Nong chao er* can mean a number of things depending on the context. Simply put it can mean 'children of the tide', 'fooling with the tide' or 'playing with the tide'. But it can also mean 'inducing an orgasm'. The sexual implications immediately indicates that 'children' or 'boy' is not an age-related term, but a reference to the roots and activities of the *nong chao er*. Further, it can be inferred as 'activating the tide' as if the *nong chao er* were capable of controlling the wave (perhaps from a spiritual or religious perspective, thus their link to Buddhism in the Qiongzhu Temple), or forming revolutions and quite literally 'overturning a dynasty'. And today in Chinese business when someone is called a '*nong chao er*' it means they take risks with style and flare. Links with wave-riding here are irresistible. Perhaps the *nong chao er* were fisherman or barge pilots by trade, but I was only just beginning to scratch the surface of their cultural significance. Were they China's first wave-riders?

兒, *er*
Children
Oracle bone script

CHAPTER TEN

A SONG
FROM SOUTH
OF THE RIVER

By the afternoon in Venice's Ca' Foscari library I was fired up to continue researching *nong chao er*. Among the many literary appearances of each term, the dictionaries reported three times when all three characters appeared together. The oldest was written in 800 AD by poet Li Yi (750-830) during the Tang dynasty (618-907). I easily translated the title, 'A Song from South of the River', and could see the last three words '*nong chao er*'. But the 17 remaining characters were more challenging. Thankfully this short song (曲 *qǔ*) is contained in a famous anthology called *Three Hundred Tang Poems* first compiled in 1763 by Sun Zhu. I had spent hours using the anthology for my literature exams and knew it had been extensively studied in the West, influencing poets such as Ezra Pound (who in turn influenced many great writers including Bruce Chatwin). I went to the librarian and requested a translated version. He presented me a rare Taiwanese version dated 1973 with translations by the great English sinologist Professor Innes Herdan.

Three Hundred Tang Poems is a classic in the Chinese education system. The most famous poems from Li Bai (my favourite), Du Fu and Bai Zhuyi are the Chinese equivalent of Dante, Lord Byron, Samuel Taylor Coleridge and Saint-John Perse. They are still learned by heart in schools throughout China today and used as an exercise guide for calligraphy lessons. Even the first Chinese heavy metal band, *Tang Dynasty Music Band* (formed in 1989), took its name from *Three Hundred Tang Poems*. I had come to know them through audio tapes I smuggled home from trips to Beijing. Their tunes fused Led Zeppelin-style distorted guitars with traditional ethnic composition, and they sang of a new tide, bringing forth diversity and freedom.

But the Tang is more than the name of a metal band and pile of poetry. To contemporary Chinese, the Tang dynasty is synonymous with grandeur and open-mindedness. Under the reign of emperor Xuan Zong (712-756) China had become 'the Middle Kingdom' at the global forefront of civilisation, art and science. Economic administration under the Tang allowed widespread prosperity. While Europe was fragmented, sieged by Arab pirates from the south and Viking raiders from the north, Tang emperors successfully ruled 80 million people, spanning from Korea to Persia, from Kazakhstan to central Vietnam. Chan An (modern day Xi An) became the largest, richest and most cosmopolitan capital of the time. The great trade routes between Central and Eastern Asia crystallised into the Silk Road. Tea, paper, silk and spices moved along these various routes all the way to the streets of Venice. And so did Buddhism, Zoroastrism, Nestorianism, Islam and Judaism. Tang rulers were progressive and enlightened, banning the death penalty, and encouraging cultural exchange. The arts flourished, and poetry was paramount. China hosts the world's oldest tradition of poetry, but during the Tang, poetry was no longer just the realm of the elite and educated. Poetry started to transcend social strata to become a recreational and artistic activity enjoyed by all classes. Poems were read aloud accompanied by music performances. Poems were a means of self-expression. And poetry was a compulsory subject at the national exams. The best poets, like Li Bai, Du Fu and Bai Zhuyi, were the rockstars of the day. But men and women of all backgrounds were involved in writing, performing and studying poetry. And today you could spend a lifetime studying Tang poetry. In fact, the *Complete Tang Poems* complied by Cao Yin (and commissioned in 1705 under the Qing dynasty) contain 49,000 poems from more than 2,200 poets.

Poet Li Yi lived at the end of the most refined period of this Tang dynasty. He was originally from the frigid northwestern ridges of Gansu, but after his success at the court exam (no doubt including some poetry analysis), he was dispatched to Luoyang in Henan province, south of the Yangtze River. He fell in love with this area, but was often sent away working as a high ranking civil servant commanding troops on the western territories of Shaanxi province. He wrote what was known as 'border poetry', a genre popular among dignitaries, like himself, managing the troops, far from the capital Chan An. He explored a longing for home and the hardships and glories of soldiers sent to fight at the outposts of the empire, in journeys that often had no return. But Li Yi was not one of the 'rockstars' of Tang poetry, and consequently only three of his poems are contained in the anthology, compared to the 34 of Li Bai or 39 of Du Fu.

Among Li Yi's three poems, 'A Song from South of the River' is the earliest occurrence I found of *nong chao er*. Here it is:

jiāngnán qǔ   lǐ yì

江 南 曲 - 李 益

A Song from South of the River by Li Yi

jià dé qútáng jiǎ   zhāozhāo wù qiè qī

嫁 得 瞿 塘 賈　　朝 朝 誤 妾 期

I married a merchant from Qutang,
But day after day he breaks his trust.

zǎo zhīcháo   yǒu xìn   jià yǔ nòngcháo ér.

早 知 潮 有 信　嫁 與 弄 潮 兒.

Had I known how faithful were the tides,
I would have married a nong chao er.

The title 'South of the River' refers to the territories south of the Yangtze, a region frequently celebrated in poems for its natural beauty. Places like Hangzhou's West Lake and Suzhou's canals still attract millions of visitors every year and were just as popular in the Tang dynasty. These are the birthplaces of southern Chinese culture. And the Yangtze and its eight tributaries are the liquid backbone of this geopolitical environment. They form an ever-changing web of rivers and canals, 5,000 km of waterways linking the East China Sea with the Tibetan plateau, the westbound Silk Road, and the northern capitals.

Just a few centuries before the Tang, the Sui dynasty (581-618) had unified Northern and Southern China and expanded pre-existing waterways into the Grand Canal, a 1,776 km long manmade river (still today the longest on the planet and a UNESCO World Heritage site) linking Beijing with a dozen major towns, all the way to Hangzhou in the south. Up to five million men and women were employed in the construction, and new routes of food trade and movement of people opened up. By the time Li Yi was describing this river scene, Tang emperors had made the north-south axis of the Grand Canal even more efficient. Produce from the southern regions, mainly rice and salt, could now be shipped north at speed for the use of the army, and a new merchant class was emerging. Conversely, intellectuals from the north started discovering the natural beauties of the south. It soon became a 'promised land' of warm weather and dramatic landscapes.

The panorama was so impressive it had, of course, to be celebrated in art. Not surprisingly these centuries marked the beginning of Chinese landscape painting, with cloud capped karst mountain peaks, solitary pine forests and rumbling rapids becoming a trade mark for centuries to come.

Li Yi himself was enchanted by the emotive scenes 'South of the River', and his poem is all about a yearning for love and home, centred around a lady contemplating the river. She is thinking of her husband, a merchant from Qutang (in modern-day Siquan province), who is likely often away working in the new world of national river trade. The first couplet depicts her sad mood. '(嫁得瞿塘賈 *jiade qutang jia)* I married a merchant from Qutang,' she says, '(朝朝誤妾期 *zhaozhao wu qie qi*) But day after day he breaks his trust.' She is complaining about a need for attention. 'Daily failing to keep his word' could be another translation of '朝朝誤妾期 *zhaozhao wu qie qi*'. Li Yi introduces her emotional state using the assonance between the word tide (潮 *chao*) and day / time (朝 *zhao*). The sexual reference is obvious to all Chinese speakers. Not only is her husband failing to make her happy, keeping her waiting, but he also misses all the 'good times' happening during his absence. Is she having an affair with a *nong chao e*r? Is she also 'fooling with the tide'?

The second couplet is both a statement of regret and laced with Daoism: '(早知潮有信 *zao zhi chao you xin*), had I known how faithful were the tides,' she says, '(嫁與弄潮兒 *jia yu nong chao er*) I would have married a *nong chao er*.' 'Had I known that the tide is so reliable,' is another valid translation of '早知潮有信 *zao zhi chao you xin*'. The word 'tide' here, with all its aftertaste of 'wave', 'revolution' and 'orgasm', is used again in the third verse. The word 信 *xin* translatable with 'trustful / reliable', refers to the flow of nature, that unstoppable ever changing force to which human beings, according to Daoist philosophy, can only conform. The predictability of the tide contrasts with the unreliability of the merchant.

While Daoism is about a return to the rhythms and presences of nature, Confucianism is about the polite and obedient citizen. The traditional Confucian order embodies strict hierarchy, based on a series of relationships so that everybody knows how to behave with respect towards each other. At the time the merchant class was just emerging (facilitated by the Grand Canal) and seen as inferior to other social classes (their status rising in later dynasties). A *nong chao er* (be it a river barge pilot, a fisherman or a wave-rider) would most likely constitute a valid alternative to a merchant, that although also from a poorer background, would be higher up in the Confucian social pyramid, and (in the spirit of the poem) know how to make a young lady happy.

Although the poem does not mention the actual act of riding the tide, if that is what the *nong chao er* did, this could be the first reference to a culture of 'wave-riders' in any literary work, preceding western occurrences of the word 'surfing' by thousands of years. But who were these 'children of the tide' and what were they actually doing on waves? Were they just swimming, bellyboarding, or standing up like the depiction from the Qiongzhu Temple in the 1880s suggests?

The second piece of literature to reference the *nong chao er* takes us from 'South of the River' to precisely the Qiantang River (or Zhe Jiang) and the act of riding the river bore. In a section called 'Zhejiang' of the 'Illustrated Memorandum of Yuanhe prefectures and Counties' written between 813-814, Tang dynasty official Li Jifu (758-814) states that: 'The river waves raises every day and every night... when it is big the wave can reach several Zhang (1 Zhang = 10 feet), and every year on the 18th day of the 8th lunar month men and women from several hundred households gather to look at boat people and fishermen face the surge and confront the waves. And they call this *nong chao*'. The context of the *nong chao er* is clear in this reference. They are 'boat people' and 'fishermen' who 'confront the waves'. But it's poetry that brings their description to life, and the third appearance of all three characters is in a poem by Pan Lang in 1009 called 'Written on the tune of Jiuquan', substantiating Li Jifu's earlier reference of the *nong chao er* riding the tide.

Although his date of birth and death are unknown, we do know that Pan Lang was a doctor living in the Hangzhou area during the Northern Song dynasty (960-1127). The Tang dynasty had collapsed, paving the way for the Song. The exact causes of the collapse of the Tang is debated, but, put simply, during the late Tang more and more power was left in the hands of regional military governors. Several internal rebellions weakened the imperial government so by the 10th century the governors were effectively independent from the central government. Add to this further political in-fighting, natural disasters and floods, and the so-called 'Five Dynasties and Ten Kingdoms' period bridged the end of the Tang in 907 and the beginning of the Song in 960. The Song's new capital was in Bianjing (modern-day Kaifeng, now in Henan province).

Pan Lang's poem takes inspiration from the Tang masters in style, and 'Jiuquan' in the tile refers to a Tang dynasty tune often used as a base to recite poems:

jiǔ quánzi *pānlàng*
酒泉子 - 潘阆.

Written on the tune of Jiuquan by Pan Lang

chángyì guāncháo *mǎn guō rén zhēngjiāng shàng wàng*
長憶觀潮　滿郭人爭江上望

I often remember the spectacle of the tide,
When everyone in town hurries to the river eager to watch.

lái yí cāng hǎi jìn chéngkōng *wànmiàn gǔshēng zhōng*
來疑滄海盡成空　萬面鼓聲中

When it arrives, it feels as if the whole ocean has drained empty,
Amid the sound of countless steel drums.

nòngcháoér xiàng tā tóu lì *shǒu bǎ hóng qí qí bù shī*
弄潮兒向濤頭立　手把紅旗旗不濕

The nong chao er go towards the head of the wave and stand up,
They hold a red flag that never gets wet.

bié lái jǐ xiàng mèng zhōng kàn *mèngjué shàng xīn hán*
別來幾向夢中看　夢覺尚心寒

I have dreamt this view many times,
And when I wake up my heart is still shocked.

Pan Lang is watching a show, or better, a spectacle, attended by almost everyone in the town of Hangzhou. The show's *pri-*

ma donna is the tidal wave itself and the *nong chao er* riding it. The verb used for 'contemplating' 觀 *guān* and contained in the first line can mean 'to watch', 'to study', or an 'empirical investigation of phenomenon'. *'Guan'* is the way Daoists 'study' nature, by immersing in it and 'contemplating' all its forms. The character depicts a man, looking at a bird, possibly a heron. It's a character also described in the 說文 Shuōwén, a famous dictionary compiled during the Han dynasty (206 BC - 22 AD) as 'carefully inspecting'. Not surprisingly Daoist temples are also called *'guan'* (for example Beijing's 白雲觀 *Báiyúnguān* Temple of the White Cloud) as if those structures, often immersed in nature, were observation stations to 'study nature', not mere places of worship.

Again, Pan Lang's description is laced with the Daoist components of science, poetry and meditation. The wave is probably arriving just after a spring low tide (when the gravitational force of the moon and sun are aligned), when 'it feels as if the whole ocean has drained empty'. Pan Lang reports that the sound of the coming 'tidal wave' is like 'countless steel drums' as if marking the beginning of a military parade. In another poem Pan Lang describes the terrifying sound of the wave as '(处处水潺潺 *chùchù shuǐ chánchán)* rumbling water everywhere'. Amid this apparent mayhem the *nong chao er* appear and 向 *xiàng* 'go towards' or 'turn towards' the head of the wave: '(弄潮兒向濤頭立 *nongchaoer xiang taotou li)* and stand up'.

Bingo. The verb 立 *li* leaves no room for confusion. The meaning has remained constant from the oracular bones to modern Chinese. It depicts a wide shouldered person standing upright on something flat. And it suddenly struck me those simple five strokes are nearly identical to Hawaiian pictograms of surfing.

132   Hawaiian pictogram
of a surfer

立, *li*
To stand
Oracle bone script

Although Hawaiians had no written language, their cultural boom between the 11th and 12th century did leave visual evidence through stone engravings. Their depiction of a surfer is nearly identical.

The character 立 *li* is clearly a person standing up on a plank. But no word in the poem is used to describe the craft they ride. The 'wave', on the other hand, offers more hints. The term is not the modern-day Chinese for 'wave' (浪 *làng*), 'breaker' (波 *bō*) or 'swell' (湧 *yǒng*), but a word I had not encountered before: 濤 *tāo*. *Tao's* right part 壽 *shòu* means 'long life' and is commonly used as a blessing, often brushed on red paper and hung outside front doors at New Year. Its form indicates an old man holding onto his walking stick in front of a ploughed field. Is this a reference to the life span of this wave, roaming the river for nearly 100 km, in a process that lasts several hours? There is nothing in the dictionaries to answer this. Nonetheless, it seems that both during the Tang and Song dynasties the word 濤 *tao* was used to depict 'big breaking waves'. Song poet Su Shi (1037-1101) uses *tao* to describe '驚濤拍岸 *jīngtāo pāiàn* frightened waves breaking on the shore' while later authors coupled it with 'snow' 雪 *xuě* to indicate '雪濤 *xuetao* cascading mountains of white water'.

Although Pan Lang's poem makes no mention of what craft the *nong chao er* are standing on, he does report that 'they hold a red flag' and apparently ride so skilfully that it 'never gets wet'. Although not certain, this seems to support the idea of riding upright, not prone, on some sort of canoe, barge, or board.

Sports flourished under the Song. Food surplus, social mobility and free time had allowed 'physical nourishments' (体育 *tǐyù*) to be widespread. Such activities included ball games, track and field, mountaineering, body-building, archery and swimming. Team sports such as 蹴鞠 *cùjū*, a ball game similar to soccer originally used as army training, and 馬球 *mǎqiú*, a form of polo originated among Tibetan horsemen, were organised into leagues and played professionally by men and women. Physical activities, such as gymnastics, martial arts and dragon-boat races, had important social functions, especially during the 11th and 12th century. Could wave-riding by the *nong chao er* be part of this culture?

"*Andemo andemo! Xe ora!* (Let's go, let's go! Time's up!)" said the librarian in a loud, booming voice, bringing me right back to the present. It was six o'clock and the library was closing. I had spent a whole day chasing waves on paper, through books and journals. I had a pile of dictionaries and photocopies spread across the desk. The dots on my map had grown in number, but the line that linked them was still blurred. However, it did now point to a precise area and era: Hangzhou, Zhejiang province of the Tang and Song, along the banks of the Qiantang River and the tidal waves that kisses them.

CHAPTER TEN — A SONG FROM SOUTH OF THE RIVER

CHAPTER ELEVEN

CONTEMPLATING THE TIDE

Over the following year my surf exploration continued to travel from poetry to Chinese history, across books, through websites and back again to Ca' Foscari's library in Venice. From the accounts by Li Yi and Pan Lang that first document *nong chao er* in poetry, across the two dynasties of the Tang and the Song, the activity had clearly developed into a major annual event at the Mid-Autumn (or Bore-Watching) Festival during the equinox tide, the largest of the year.

But of course, I was only scratching the surface. In over 5,000 years of history, China has produced more written accounts than any other civilisation on the planet, starting with the oracular bones of the Shang dynasty. But during the turbulent unification of the empire under the Qin (220 - 206 BC), emperor Qingshi tried to eradicate most of the previous culture by burning precious texts and executing intellectuals. Thankfully, under the peaceful and prosperous reign of the Han (206 BC - 220 AD), a court astrologer named Sima Qian (135 - 86 BC) embraced the mission of reconstructing 2,500 years of historical records, from the Shang (1600 - 1047 BC), Xia (2070 - 1600 BC) and Zhou (1047 - 256 BC) dynasties, all the way to the Han. Qian's monumental work known as *Shiji* (*The Records of the Grand Historian*) set the precedent for the following 24 dynasties. Consequently, the amount of biographies, battles accounts, festival descriptions, court diaries, ethnographies and geopolitical notes that exist in Chinese history is overwhelming. When historian Sima Guang (1019-1086) and a team of specialists complied the epic *Zizhi Tongijan (Universal History)* during the reign of the Northern Song (960-1127) the works filled two huge rooms in the imperial library, contained 294 volumes and over three million characters. And that was 900 years ago. Casting light on something as obscure as the *nong chao er* through literary analysis is no mean feat!

The Northern and Southern Song dynasties are extremely important in relation to *nong chao er* because they were a time of continued cultural and economic expansion. Also, book printing techniques invented during the Tang were developed further. Consequently, what had previously been considered 'high culture' - court poetry, Buddhist sutras, theatre, plays and folk novels - became cheaper to produce and more widely available to a broader audience, transcending further across the social strata than it did in the Tang. The shift also facilitated a new wave of 'independent' historians, publishing in unofficial accounts.

During the Song, art and science also continued to thrive. This period saw the invention of the magnetic compass and the development of evolution theory, while the polymath Su Song (1020-1101) pioneered ideas on time and the universe. With big urban populations, the Song was a more free and vibrant society than the Tang. While the Tang had curfews in towns and cities, the Song fostered the buzz of nightlife and eating became the great ritual it is today. 'People should be well fed' was a motto, and the first restaurant culture in the world was born. There were even self-help guide books about sex and senescence. And the new rising class were merchants, once considered bottom of the Confucian order, but now climbing through the ranks.

The most comprehensive account of the Song is *History of the Song* compiled (by a number of authors) after the fall of the dynasty by the Mongol regency of the Yuan (1271-1368). But most of the

496 chapters have not been translated in any western language. Navigating such an opus in its printed form I was only floating on the skin on this vast ocean of text. But by 'surfing' the net I could really make progress. Of course, from a western perspective the Chinese internet is demonised as being censored and blocked to American-owned social media sites and search engines, thus limiting freedom of speech and independent research. But the western media often fails to report how exhaustive and efficient the Chinese internet is to a Chinese speaking and reading audience. Search engines like baidu.com (the Chinese equivalent to Google) are staggering: complete historical works are published online and highly accessible through searching for key words.

My first baidu.com search for *nong chao er* delivered over eight million linked pages. But the interesting results arrived when I combined key words found in the poems. The first breakthrough was coupling 红旗 *hóngqí* (red flag) and *nong chao er*, then followed up by looking in books. I found an article called 'Contemplating the Tide' (觀潮 *guanchao*) in *Recollections of Wulin Garden* - a miscellany of 筆記 *biji* or 'brush notes' written around 1290 by late Song, early Yuan author 周密 Zhou Mi (1231-1298) and reprinted in 1984 by the Zhejiang People's Press. In contrast to the official histories focused on dignitaries and state affairs, 'brush notes' are based on personal experiences. During the Song, these tales often took the shape of novellas depicting everyday life in bustling cities and eye witness descriptions of sporting events, theatre shows and social spaces. The author Zhou Mi was from the northern province of Shandong, birthplace of Confucius, and had fled south with his family after Mongol Kublai Khan (1215-1294) had invaded from the north and sieged his hometown Jinan, and marched all the way to the capital Chan An (modern day Xi An). In the flight south, Hangzhou had become the new capital of the Southern Song, and now the cultural and political epicentre of the country, with the Grand Canal able to transport people to enjoy big events. 'Wulin Garden' was located next to the new imperial palace in Hangzhou, where intellectuals spent time drinking tea, discussing ideas and sharing stories.

The episode 'Contemplating the Tide' describes the Mid-Autumn Festival. The event - originally a celebration of the harvest between late September and early October, during autumn's first full moon - had now evolved into a cultural appreciation of the moon and moon watching (also known as the Bore-Watching Festival). It continues to this day with 'mooncakes' (round pastries filled with cream and dried fruit and decorated with Mandarin characters for 'roundness' and 'reunion') distributed as gifts. The alignment of the moon and sun creates the biggest tidal range of the year, generating waves up to 5 meters high in the estuary of the Qiantang River.

Back in 1009, when Pan Lang wrote his poem, the capital was based in Bianjing, on the banks of the Yellow River, a few hundred kilometres north. In those days of the Northern Song, reigning Emperor Taizong (976-997), the second since the founding of the dynasty, was too concerned with the recent unification and pacifying the northern tribes to attend what was likely a 'local custom' in a southern city. Zhou Mi's account, however, describes the wave-riding parade at its apex, during the decadent years of Emperor Duzong (1264-1274) just before the final collapse of the Southern Song (imposed by Mongol Kublai Khan). By now in the capital Hangzhou the show had been elevated to great significance. And the Emperor was there to watch the spectacle. The North had already fallen and the Mongols were pushing at the borders. Emperor Duzong had delegated all state affairs to the hands of Jia Sidao, his maverick brother, and lived a life of leisure and opulence. The court had simply given up trying to fend off the Mongols, and was going down in style before they arrived.

guān cháo   *z h ō u m ì*
觀潮 - 周密

Contemplating the Tide by Zhou Mi

The tidal bore on the Zhejiang (the Qiantang) is one of the great wonders of the world. It reaches its full force from the 15th to the 18th day of the 8th moon. When it begins to rise far away at the Ocean Gate, it only resembles a silver thread. But as it gradually approaches, it transforms into a wall of jade and white capped mountains, swallowing the sky and inundating the sun. Its gigantic roar is as loud as thunder, exploding and rising up with extreme power worthy of brave heroes. The great poet Yang Chenghai described 'silver waves as big as city walls traversing the river and breaking like jade belts'.

As in every year, the governor of the capital appears at the Zhejiang Pavilion to inspect the navy. Warships in the hundreds are arrayed along both banks. Suddenly, they all rush to divide into battalions of five. At the same time the cavalry wave flags, performing with fire-weapons and swords on the water as if standing on firm land. Then yellow smoke rises on all sides, and people can barely see each other. The explosions on the water are deafening and earth-shaking, as if mountains are collapsing. When the smoke disperses and the assault has ended, there is not a trace of a hull: all the 'enemy ships' have been burned by fire and disappeared under the waves.

Then hundreds of brave watermen from Wu, with unfastened hair and tattoos, holding ten coloured flags, race to the water at the sound of drums. They paddle against the flow, towards the oncoming waves, appearing and disappearing among the leviathan waves ten thousand ren (1 ren = 2.66 metres) long. Then they leap up, and perform a hundred manoeuvres without getting the tail of their flags even slightly wet. This is how they show off their skill. Hence the nobles reward them with silver prizes.

Up and down along the river banks for 10 li (5 km), pearls, jade, gauze and silk flood the eyes, and horses and carriages clog the roads. Every kind of food and drink costs double the normal price, and yet, where viewing tents are rented out, not a bit of ground is left for even a mat. The palace watches the scene, as customary. From this high terrace, the bird's-eye view makes it all appear as if in the palm of one's hand, like contemplating an open-air painting. The people of the capital gaze up at the yellow canopies and pheasant feathers (Emperor and Empress) flying high among the nine clouds. It is like the island of Peng-lai (Heaven on Earth) caressed by the sound of the flute.

The description of the surge approaching Hangzhou is un-equivocal. Outside of the 'Ocean Gate' (city harbour), towards the east, says the author, the tidal wave 'only resembles a silver thread' of unbroken water. But it rises up quickly just before entering the city centre, turning from 'silver lines' of unbroken waves to 'white capped mountains', a clear sign of a breaking river bore. The image of 'silver waves' and 'jade' is reinforced in the work of a more famous writer called Yang Chenghai, considered one of the greats of Song poetry. Waves 'as big as city walls' would be between four and six metres, but of course this could be an exaggeration of the actual size. Zhou Mi described the wave as loud as 'thunder' (雷霆 *léitíng*) and being 'worthy of brave heroes'. Serendipitously, the Chinese name given to me by Professor Yang, 建豪 *Jiànháo*, meaning 'valiant hero' or 'healthy hero', contains the same character used by Zhou Mi for 'worthy of brave heroes' - 雄豪 *xióngháo*. I was deeper and more connected than ever in the translations. As 'Contemplating the Tide' continued, the mighty Song navy had gathered - possibly setting sail from the nearby island of Zhoushan, where it was stationed - to be inspected by the Emperor and the highest dignitaries in a parade. Water parades were common during the Song dynasty, often performed on the West Lake, a fresh water reservoir in Hangzhou.

Notable Song writers, including Wu Zimu (in his *Mengliang* 143
Lu, Dreaming over a Millet Bowl) have also described water parades in the late 13th century taking place 'on the eighth day of
the second moon' when crowds circled the West Lake to witness
the 'dragons battle' where six boats decorated as dragons faced
each other in various rounds, with the crews armed with long
poles, competing to push the rival crews into the water. At its
zenith the Song army included over one million units, with the
navy representing its most advanced department. Massive warships were capable of transporting more than 1,000 soldiers.
The boats on display in Zhou Mi's description are called 艨艟
méng chōng and represented the cutting edge technology of the
time. They were agile, powered by rowers and covered with a
leather hide, impenetrable to arrows, with holes for crossbows
and spears. During the parade, *meng chong* simulated an assault
on enemy vessels. The cavalry was there as well, possibly operating on floating barges, storming forward 'as if standing on
firm land'.

A massive crowd was witnessing from the nearby hills and river banks, and Zhou Mi was among the dignitaries positioned on
the top floor of the Zhejiang Pavilion, close to the Liuhe Pagoda
(Six Harmonies Pagoda) that still stands at the foot of the Yuelun
Hill, facing the Qiantang River in southern Hangzhou today.

The staged assault started at the signal of gunpowder fire,
exclusive to China at the time. 9th century Daoist alchemists developed gunpowder while searching for the elixir of life. It was
first used in warfare in 1000 AD, but did not spread to Eurasia
until the end of the 13th century. Several kinds of explosives were
reported in battle accounts and staged assaults at the time, including bombs, shells and grenades. In Zhou Mi's account the
mock enemy vessels were set ablaze, while the army paraded
with fire-weapons and swords.

CHAPTER ELEVEN – CONTEMPLATING THE TIDE

Thanks to precise tide charts, the staged assault was just before the arrival of the tidal wave. The account reaches a crescendo: 'Then hundreds of brave watermen from Wu, with unfastened hair and tattoos (吳兒善泅者數百 *Wú ér shàn qiú zhě shùbǎi* 皆披髮文身 *jiē pīfǎ wén shēn*), holding 10 coloured flags, race to the water at the sound of drums (手持十幅大彩旗 *shǒuchí shí fú dà cǎiqí* 爭先鼓勇 *zhēngxiān gǔ yǒng*). They paddle against the flow, towards the oncoming waves, appearing and disappearing among the leviathan waves ten thousand *ren* long (溯迎而上 *Sù yíng ér shàng* 出沒於鯨波萬仞中 *chūmò yú jīng bō wàn rèn zhōng*). Then they leap up, and perform a hundred manoeuvres without getting the tail of their flags even slightly wet (騰身百變 *Téngshēn bǎi biàn* 而旗尾略不沾濕 *ér qíwěi lvè bù zhānshī*). This is how they show off their skill (以此誇能 *yǐ cǐ kuā néng*). Hence the nobles reward them with silver prizes. (而豪民貴宦 *Er háo mín guì huàn* 爭賞銀彩 *zhēng shǎng yín cǎi*)'.

Bingo! More evidence of *nong chao er*, and, importantly, their background. 'They paddle against the flow... leap up, and perform manoeuvres'. But who are these 'brave watermen from Wu' with 'unfastened hair and tattoos'?

CHAPTER ELEVEN — CONTEMPLATING THE TIDE

CHAPTER TWELVE

WATERMEN FROM WU

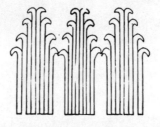

While translating Zhou Mi's 'Contemplating the Tide' I had come across 'brave watermen from Wu' riding the river bore in Hangzhou. My research continued with full force, now with a lead into the background of the *nong chao er*.

The 吳 Wú people, historically located around the Qiantang River, are renowned in Chinese history for their water skills, and commonly worked as fishermen and barge pilots. Ethnographically, the Wu (and their neighbouring 越 Yuè), are direct descendants of the Hemudu, Majiabang and Liangzhu cultures, settled in the southeastern coastline of Asia as farming fishermen and fishing farmers. Traits of their language is still recognisable in modern Chinese, including the word 'river' 江 *jiāng*. DNA research also suggests the connection between these early farming fishermen (among the first to domesticate rice) and Austronesian and Tai Kadai settlers.

This is the same ethnic group that triggered the Austronesian migration throughout the South China Sea to Polynesia and Eastern Africa starting from the second millennium BC, reaching as far as Rapa Nui in the west and Madagascar in the east. One of the world's oldest recorded boats - the 5-metre-long Kuahuqiao dugout canoe datable at around 8000 BC - was excavated in the Wu-Yue territory and is now on display at the Zhejiang museum in Hangzhou. Also in the same museum is a depiction of a man from Yue-Wu and Yue were fierce enemies but shared customs and language - dated around the 5th century BC. The tattoo patterns - stylised waves, armbands, triangular shapes - and face masks bear remarkable resemblance with Polynesian tattoos. The mask on the torso, in particular, is very similar to the Polynesian *Tiki*, gods and ancestors recurrent in the body art of all Polynesian Islands.

Man from Yue
State Museum of Zhejiang Province
500 BC

During the dynasties of the Sui (581-618) and Tang (618-907) the Wu-Yue people were scattered throughout southwest China, but most concentrated along the southeast coastline. For generations they lived in boat houses, working as fishermen or in water transportation, piloting boats and barges among both coastal waves and rive bores. And, as we discovered earlier, the first appearance of a 'tidal wave' in Chinese literature is dated 500 BC in the *History of the Southern States of Wu and Yue* compiled by Han dynasty historian Zhao Ye. The King of Wu condemned Minister Wu Zixu to death, and Wu Zixu's infuriated soul 'enraged the waters' until they 'rose in great billows causing havoc among his enemies'.

But there is a *yin* and *yang* in the reputation of the Wu-Yue people as both brilliant but reckless. Their prowess on the rivers, lakes and oceans has left both positive and negative traces in Chinese literature from the end of the Neolithic period (2000 BC) onwards. While Tang dynasty official Li Jifu (758-814) simply described the Wu as 'boat people' and 'fishermen' in practical terms, Song calligrapher, poet and dignitary Su Dongpo (also known as Su Shi - 1037-1110) described the Wu as 'over familiar with waves and deep water [...] they bravely commit suicide and don't value their lives'. Further, another Song poet, Ren Xun (1133-1204), wrote in 'Contemplating the tide from Zhejiang Pavilion' (a near-identical title to Zhou Mi) that 'Wu kids learn to play with the tides since they are young' but 'they consider their lives as light as goose feathers'. The metaphor is a reference to how they skirt danger with reckless abandon. I could picture modern-day big wave riders being described in the same way by a disapproving public.

Song dynasty writer Wu Zimu (in *Mengliang Lu, Dreaming over a Millet Bowl*) described the Wu as, 'rascals [...] who don't value their own life'. Wu Zimu wrote, 'among the people in

Hangzhou, there are some rascals who don't value their own life, and set out using big coloured flags, or small red and green parasol umbrellas, or with a pole mounted with coloured satin, anticipating the full tide and heading to the river mouth'.

Then came a breakthrough that fired me up - the description by Wu Zimu of 'treading waves, 踏浪 *tà làng*: 'In a group of about a hundred, they hold a flag and tread waves to enjoy the practice of playing with the tide. Some hold five small flags, move on the tide's head and play tricks'. Su Shi also used the term treading waves in a poem titled 瑞鹧鸪 *Ruì Zhègū*, 'Auspicious Partridge' describing, 'a small red flag in the shadow of emerald mountains, I'm a wave-treading boy from Jiangnan (South of the River)'. A further ethnographic account of the Wu-Yue people comes from Song poet Yang Wanli (1127-1206) - one of the most prominent (and nationalistic) poets of the time. In a poem called 蛋民 *Dàn Mín* Boat People, Yang Wanli describes how the Wu 'learn to tread waves from a very young age'.

There is clearly great reverence for the skills of the Wu-Yue people at the time of the Tang and Song dynasties, and the art of 'wave treading' is a commonly used term to describe their technique. Perhaps these are the 'hundred manoeuvres' described by Zhou Mi. In another section of *Recollections of Wulin Garden* Zhou Mi also references 'treading waves' and, even more revealing, mentions that they ride on drifting wood, and compares the Wu to Buddhist monks: *'Among the watermen in town, there are some that resemble Buddhist monks. They gather in a group of a hundred, holding coloured flags, and compete in treading waves. They head straight to the river mouth to welcome the tide. Moreover there's some who tread on drifting wood, tossed around by the water like puppets, performing hundreds of water tricks, having fun, each displaying great mastery'.*

Clearly, these brave young men from Wu-Yue are not the navy soldiers performing the staged assault, but civilian experts on the river. As the tidal wave approaches, 'they head straight to the river mouth to welcome the tide (直到海门迎潮 *zhídào hǎimén yíng cháo)*' as if they are willing to offer their lives to placate the river, perhaps inspiring Zhou Mi to compare them to Buddhist monks, drawing parallels with the *Luohan* of the Qiongzhu Temple.

When riding the tidal wave, the *nong chao er* are 'performing hundreds of water tricks (水百戏 *shuǐ bǎi xì),* having fun (撮弄等 *cuō nòng dǎng),* each displaying great mastery (各呈伎艺 *gè chéng jì yì)'*. There is a clear difference between the 'hundred manoeuvres (百變 *bai bian)* 'described earlier by Zhou Mi and the 'hundred water tricks (水百戏 *shui bai xi)*' described here. The first reference revolves around the word 變 *bian* that means 'mutation', 'transformation' or 'sudden movement', without much 'fun' or 'play' involved. So 'a hundred manoeuvres' could also be translated as 'a hundred movements'. In contrast 'a hundred water tricks' revolves around the word 戏 *xi*, that implies 'a movement done for fun', 'play', 'a game' or 'trickery'. Thus 'tricks' is a good translation.

But the big revelation is in Zhou Mi's preceding line where, 'There's some who tread on drifting wood, tossed around by the water like puppets (又有踏混木 *yòu yǒu tà hùn mù* 水傀儡 *shuǐ kuǐlěi)'*. This is the first reference to a craft. Previously, even though there are numerous references to the poles and flags held whilst riding the river bore by the *nong chao er*, you could infer that they were swimming and bodysurfing without a craft. Perhaps some were, but Zhou Mi explains how some 'tread on drifting wood (踏混木 *tà hùn mù)'*. 踏 *Ta* is the verb 'to tread' (as in 踏浪 *ta lang* - tread waves) while 混木 *hun mu* can result in a number of translations, from 'uncut wood', 'rough wood' or 'drifting wood', or even 'log', 'branch' or 'pole'. Therefore this could be a reference to the plank or board they ride prone, or stand up on, or it could be a further reference to the long pole with flag already described in Zhou Mi's account.

I could only fantasise about the 'hundred manoeuvres' and 'hundred water tricks' and the intricacies of 'wave treading'. But as a surf magazine editor who regularly read poorly written accounts of surfing in the popular press that lacked the syntax of a surfer's vocabulary, I knew that these accounts might be cartoonish versions of the complexity of manoeuvres perhaps the *nong chao er* could perform and would discuss with their own detail and flair. But I was left frustrated that Zhou Mi did not describe in more detail the craft ridden by the *nong chao er,* or if they were commonly lying or standing or even bodysurfing.

The nuances of translation could lead any one of those 'translation geeks' back in Venice in a number of different directions and conclusions. But in the Qiongzhu Temple in Yunnan the *Luohan* are depicted riding upright on top of mythical animals, mostly fish (and carp to be more specific). So I began to search for the character 鱼 *yú* fish with *nong chao er* and made some new breakthroughs that shed light on Zhou Mi's reference to the *nong chao er* and 'brave watermen from Wu' as 'resembling Buddhist monks'.

The oldest mention I found that linked *nong chao er* with *fish* was contained in a poem from the late Tang dynasty author Chen Tao (824-882) called '钱塘对酒曲 *Qiántáng duì jiǔqū* Records on the Qiantang River'. Chen Tao was strongly influenced by Daoism and Buddhism, also features in the *300 Tang Poems* collection, and adds a religious context of the parades:

qiántáng duì   *chén táo*
钱塘对 - 陈陶

Records on the Qiantang River by Chen Tao

fēng tiān yàn bēi xī líng chóu
风天雁悲西陵愁

When the cold wind comes birds and people alike feel sad,

shǐ jūn hóng qí nòng tāo tóu
使君红旗弄涛头

So the commanders let the people perform
with red flags on the head of the waves.

dōng hǎi shén yú qí wèi dé
东海神鱼骑未得

They ride on the fish of the God of the Eastern Sea.

jiāng tiān dà xiào xián yōu yōu
江天大笑闲悠悠

And the atmosphere on the river becomes cheerful.

Chen Tao's reference to 'cold wind' here means both 'winter-time' and 'times of social distress'. The 'God of the Eastern Sea' - also known as the God of the Sea, the Sea Spirit 海神 *Hǎishén*, or more commonly, The Dragon God or The Dragon King 龍王 *Lóng-wáng* - has long been venerated as the water deity along all coastlines and waterways in China, and remains so to this day, often depicted encircled by waves, riding upright with a sword in hand.

海龍王 *Hailong wang*
Dragon king
Album leaf, 1850

The Dragon King is believed to regulate rain, flood and tide, phenomena that have been needed to be respected, predicted and controlled through rituals and civil engineering (in equal measure) since the earliest days of Chinese civilisation.

Temples dedicated to The Dragon King are a recurrent feature along the coasts and rivers of Zhejiang, especially on the turbulent Qiantang. Other water deities, namely the God of the Tides (潮神 *Cháo Shén*) and Spirit of the Waves (濤神 *Bō Shén*) are linked directly to the Qiantang and Minister Wu Zixu who died in 484 BC as mentioned earlier in the *History of the Southern States of Wu and Yue* compiled by Han dynasty historian Zhao Ye. Wu Zixu was a ruler of the Wu and Minister during the turbulent Warring States and Spring and Autumn period. He warned his Emperor Fu Chai that the enemy state of Yue would rise up one day to take revenge on the Wu. But the advice was ignored because Emperor Fu Chai did not trust Wu Zixu. Undermined at court, Wu Zixu was executed and his body thrown into the Qiantang, only to reveal an oncoming and destructive river bore. It was believed that the soul of Wu Zixu caused the angry tides.

Therefore, riding 'on the fish of the God of the Eastern Sea' would certainly be the domain of extremely skilled and revered people. Similar descriptions of fish-inspired craft being ridden by the men from Wu come from Xin Qiji (1140-1207) in 'Fishermen and Tide Watchers in front of Prime Minister Ye'. Xin Qiji was a poet living five decades before Zhou Mi still under the Southern Song. His poem offers further illumination onto the riding abilities of the *nong chao er*, who were not only performing manoeuvres, water tricks and treading waves, but dancing.

mō yú ér   guāncháoshang y è chéngxiàng   xīn q ì j í

摸鱼儿 观潮上叶丞相 - 辛弃疾

Fishermen and Tide Watchers
in front of Prime Minister Ye by Xin Qiji

wú ér bù pà jiāolóng n ù

吴儿不怕蛟龙怒

Young men from Wu are not afraid of the fury of the flood dragon.

fēngbō píng bù

风波平步

They dominate wind and waves.

kàn hóng pèi jīng fēi

看红旆惊飞

Look at their swallow tailed red flag fly,

tiào yú zhí shang

跳鱼直上

They jump up on the flying fish.

c ù t à lànghuā w ǔ

蹙踏浪花舞

Stomping and treading they dance on the wave foam.

The 'brave watermen from Wu' here are not simply riding the waves, they are doing it in style. They are dancing. The character 舞 *wǔ* is also used by Zhou Mi in *Recollections of Wulin Garden* 60 times, often combined with 歌 *gē* (singing). The word *wu* is still used today in its modern meaning of 'dancing'. The original character carved on the oracular bones of the Shang dynasty shows a shaman, performing leaps, walking up and down in codified movements and holding one ox tail in each hand.

Again, there are immediate parallels with Hawaii, where surfing festivals were used to celebrate the deity *Lono*, associated with fertility, agriculture, rainfall, music and peace. A fusion of sporting competition, religious practice and public gathering was clearly referenced in all these poems. Another author from Zhejiang province called Gao Zhu (1170-1241) reinforces the competitive nature of these events in a poem called 'Watching the Return from the Tide Session' where, 'After their session they go back to town. Red victorious flags are flying high. White defeated flags are down'. But importantly, the watermen are 'received in the central road of town at the sound of drums'. The competitive nature of the river performance is confirmed by Zhou Mi's reference to the 'silver prizes', and of course the religious significance with the references to placate the various gods and spirits of the river, tide and sea.

In Zhou Mi's closing paragraph to 'Contemplating the Tide' the social importance of the show is also clear. The social strata were stretched out on the river banks to watch the show. Moving around was almost impossible. The roads were blocked with chariots, street stalls selling food and the Emperor and Empress were there to watch the show. Zhou Mi referred to the Emperor and Empress using religious symbols 'yellow canopies and pheasant feathers flying high among the nine clouds'. They were not simply 'watching', they were absorbing the energy of the view, soaking in its spiritual significance, or, in the words of the title, 'Contemplating the Tide'. And the 'brave watermen from Wu' were willing to sacrifice themselves to the waves, placate the fury of the gods, and, of course, put on a thrilling show, so spectacular it was like 'the island of Peng-lai'. This was not a reference to *Pangu* the creator, nor to modern Penghu Island in Taiwan, but the mythical dwelling of the immortals known as Pengdao supposedly in Shandong province, and considered 'heaven on Earth'.

CHAPTER TWELVE — WATERMEN FROM WU

CHAPTER THIRTEEN

THE RISE AND FALL OF WAVE TREADING

As my research continued it was clear that the *nong chao* er and their revered practice of 踏浪 *ta lang* (wave treading) was highly active on the Qiantang during the Tang and the Song, from the Tang poetry of Bai Zhuyi (772-846) and Northern Song poetry of Su Shi (1037-1110) to the Mid-Autumn Festivals of the Southern Song, with all the trademark references to the skills of 'a hundred manoeuvres' and 'water tricks', 'raising flags' and 'playing with tide' and even 'dance'. But throughout the descriptions, there was great attention to the danger (and sometimes tragedy) of the practice. The *nong chao* er threatened their lives every time they faced the head of the tide, and ultimately this was too much for the strictly Confucian codes of dynastic China.

After witnessing several fatal accidents among tide-players, in 1065 Hangzhou governor Cai Xiang (1012-1067) promoted the first recorded ban against the activity. A document by Cai Xiang entitled '戒弄潮文 *Jiè nòngcháo wén* Quit playing with the tide' reads: 'Some swimmers partake in riding the tide, and accidentally throw the body given to them by their parents to the abysses, where fishes and dragons roam. They sink and drown to boast their ability. They send their soul straight to the underworld, their wives and kids crying and staring at the water surface. Their life comes to an end, but not according to natural fate; they die without being mourned, disrespecting human relations, causing unbearable pain. So, in all occasion of spectacular tides this year, watching the tide will be allowed as per consuetude. But if commoners or soldiers will brave the tidal wave, they will be punished'.

Despite Cai Xiang's emphasis on the apparent stupidity, futility and policing of the practice, there is no evidence of the *nong chao er* being caught and punished. Perhaps there was a thriving underground movement of riding the tide in secret in the same way that Hawaiians rode waves in secret when colonising European missionaries repressed the activity?

Nevertheless, in the turbulent 100 years that followed Cai Xiang's ban, with the empire under siege from the Mongols, the practice of riding the tide apparently peaked in popularity, as we have seen in Zhou Mi's account, as an event witnessed by the Emperor himself, capable of bringing joy to the capital and diverting attention from the political tensions swallowing the Song as the Mongols swept south.

But if you think about the obvious danger of the river bore for spectators and river-side inhabitants alone, it was inevitable that the safety conscious Chinese would ultimately ban the activity. In his *Memorandum on the Sea* poet Zhu Shuzhen (1135-1180) described an event when 'typhoon produced eastern waves as big as mountains shook heaven and earth in an instant, and countless households on the sea front got washed away. And not a soul was to be found'. With so many spectators drowning when the tide came thundering down the river, the practice of riding the tide was frequently banned by officials.

During the Yuan dynasty (1271-1368) that succeeded the Song, Hangzhou was known as Kinsai by Kublai Khan and the invading Mongols. This is when Venetian Marco Polo travelled to China, describing opulent Kinsai 'with lofty bridges and exquisite buildings' and even praising local women as 'dainty and angelical creatures'.

But there are no references to the *nong chao* er by Marco Polo. Yet in the subsequent Ming dynasty (1368-1644), as catastrophic tides continued to cause havoc in Hangzhou, a few writers described the *nong chao er*, but not in reference to festivals or respect of water deities, but as outlaws. In the novel *On The Water Margin* Shi Nai'an (1296-1372) described the outlaw Zhang Sun as 'using his two legs to tread waves (自把两条腿踏着水浪 *zi ba liang tiaotui tazhe shuilang*), as if he was moving on flat land (如行平地 *ru xing pingdi*), with water not even covering his belly (那水浸不过 他肚皮 *na shuijin buguo ta duzi*), submerged only to under his navel (淹着脐下 *yanzhe qixia*)'. Clearly Zhang Sun was riding prone. Tian Rucheng (1503-1557) in *Notes About a Trip to West Lake* wrote, 'people living close to the river are good in treading waves and traversing billows, and they call this *nong chao*. Some of them in antiquity were very talented at this'. There was a clear sense by now that if the *nong chao* er were riding the tide, they were doing it in secret to avoid arrest as the practice was officially banned. By this time the safety and defence of the river was the responsibility of local officials. If there was a accident, the officials could be held responsible and put to death. The trailblazing feats of the *nong chao er* were policed to extinction.

By the Qing dynasty (1644-1912) records of the *nong chao er* have all but disappeared. The last reference to a craft being used to ride the tides can be found in *Anthology of 24 Dynastic Authors* compiled by Shao Zhangheng (1637- 1704), an imperial scholar from Jiangsu province. In *Biography of Yan Dianshi* author Shao Zhangheng describes a battle in 1641 between a horde of pirates operating on the river and the local population defending Hangzhou, led by a young official surnamed Yan. The account is written during the turbulent final years of the Ming dynasty and reports that, '*There are hundreds of pirates on the river who spread their sails and ride the tide breaking into inland areas' pillaging villages* (有江盗百艘 张帜乘潮阑入内地 *You jiang dao*

海內奇觀 *hai nei qi guan*,
Marvellous Spectacles
钱塘江图, View of the Qiantang jiang
Wood engraving, 1609

bai shou zhangzhi cheng chao lan ru neidi). The newly appointed young official Yan organised locals in a small army and fought back the outlaws with arrows and bamboo spears. An engraving from the same period titled 'View of the Qiantang Jiang' (dated 1609) confirms the use of small sailboats as a waveriding vehicle in the Hangzhou area at the time.

But there is a stark difference between this episode based during the late Ming and the previous occurrences of tide rides. The pirates did not ride the tide for fun. They did not 'fool' or 'play' (弄 *nong*) with the tide or perform a 'hundred water tricks (水百戏 *shui bai xi*) described by Zhou Mi. They did not 'tread waves' (踏浪 *ta lang*), or 'dance' 舞 *wu* on the water. They simply used the wave to their advantage and 'mounted' it. The word 'mount' used here is 乘 chéng, as in 'riding a horse'.

But of course the Qiantang River has changed dramatically since the times of Zhou Mi and the descriptions of the *nong chao er* at the Mid-Autumn Festivals. This is clear when referencing the Song cartography of *Yu Ji Tu* 'Map of the Tracks of Yu' carved on stone in 1137 and now located in the Stele Forest of Xi'an.

The map features a grid of 100 li blocks (1 li is around 500 metres). Each block is around 50 by 50 km, accurately showing China's coastline and river systems. The Bay of Hangzhou and the mouth of the Qiantang was clearly wider than today. Just east of Hangzhou, where the river is now only two kilometres wide, the coast had the shape of a vast oceanic bay divided by a short channel where the harbour was located. This is visible also on maps contained in local gazetteers from the Song dynasty.

禹跡圖 *yu ji tu*
Map of the Tracks of Yu
Stele, 1137

View of the Qiantang Jiang
Google Earth, 2019

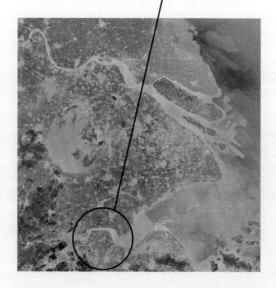

It was only more recently, after the founding of the Chinese Republic in 1949, that vast stretches of land, along both banks, were developed as agricultural areas by confining the river into a narrower, heavily walled waterway. As a result, the ocean has moved some 50 km east, and the tidal bore now starts to white-cap around 40 km further east from the city. In the times of Zhou Mi, it was most likely rising up quickly just before entering the city centre, turning from 'a silver thread' to 'white capped mountains'.

It is therefore possible to link the decline of the *nong chao er* to the increasing danger of the activity as the river was gradual-ly controlled, and the surrounding population continued to in-crease, becoming more urbanised, and making devastating floods more frequent, thus inducing a much bigger fear in the popula-tion. These changes in the delta will have certainly increased the unpredictability and ferocity of the tidal bore. The natural beach-like environment of the river would have gradually disappeared.

But the river bore is still as active as ever. There are around 100 river bores worldwide, but the Qiantang is unique in that it forms every high tide, twice a day, every day of the year. Fundamental to tidal bores are funnel shaped river-mouths and large tides at riv-er entrances. The Hangzhou delta is around 100 km wide, but the river itself, at the mouth, is just two kilometres. Coupled with the shallow, shoaling coastline, as the tide rises (up to nine metres) it pushes a massive body of water into the river, and on the biggest tides of the year this can break at one to four meters in height, travelling upstream for over 100 km at a speed of 8 to 25 km/h.

Collecting and translating this amount of work (alongside my ongoing role as editor of *SurfNews* magazine) had taken years. The more I researched this story, the more I needed to create a phys-ical link with these watermen. They were the bridge between my love of Chinese culture, surfing and the adventurous spirit of the Monkey King. It was time to plan that trip to Hangzhou, suggested all those years ago by the Abbot at the Qiongzhu Temple.

It turned out that photographer John Callahan was assembling a team to map the waves around the Shengsi and Zhoushan archipelagos, offshore from Shanghai, and outside of the Hangzhou Bay. Scoring a typhoon swell in September was the plan, and I suggested we could then travel with the same crew of professional surfers to Hangzhou to witness, then hopefully attempt to ride the river bore. It wouldn't be the biggest tide of the year during the Mid-Autumn Festival scheduled for the following month, but it should be spectacular enough.

However, we were not going to be the first foreigners to attempt to ride the Qiantang. In 1988 English surfer Stuart Matthews organised a groundbreaking expedition here with a film crew from the *BBC* and *National Geographic*. Matthews cut his teeth on the Severn Bore in England, and at that time was a world record holder, having rode the wave for over four kilometres with Welsh surfer Pete Jones. Of course, Matthews knew that the Qiantang was a different beast compared to the Severn Bore, meandering through rural Gloucestershire in England. He started researching the Qiantang on a trip in 1984, and by 1988 was armed with permits from the Haining municipality to ride what was forecast to be the biggest bore in 400 years. As a global expert, the Chinese authorities perhaps considered Matthew's request as a reconnaissance operation to run future events that could generate tourism revenue.

Stuart Matthews wrote articles for a number of surfing magazines after the trip, explaining they purchased boats, engines and safety equipment in Hong Kong. Filming started in late September 1988, but on the first outing one of the boats was consumed and capsized by a six metre high bore. It was a terrifying start and the crew named the bore 'The Silver Dragon' after seeing this three kilometres wide bubbling surge coming towards them at great speed. Despite the obvious feeling of unease, they continued the project, and the next day Matthews rode the bore. He described it as 'a cauldron of foam three meters high' and said he 'was thrown into the air and rode prone for the first 200 meters'. When the wave cleaned up Matthews got to his feet, riding for two kilometres. 'I was buzzing,' wrote Matthews, 'but the camera shots were thought to be too distant, so it was agreed to do exactly the same the following day'.

Next day, the crew were greeted with excellent conditions, this time in Hangzhou just in front of the Six Harmonies Pagoda, and Matthews caught a similar sized wave, explaining how he was 'catapulted into the air before settling in front of the breaking section'. However, the director had instructed the camera boat to get as close as possible and due to shooting on 16mm it was decided not to change the film from the previous day as stocks were running low. The boat was just metres from Matthews when it was caught by the wave. It broke in two, throwing the camera crew and driver into the river. 'I had been on my feet for only seconds when I had to abort my ride and go to the rescue of my boat driver,' wrote Matthews. The camera man and sound man were picked up by the safety boat and thankfully no-one lost their lives. Sadly the camera and both days film were swallowed by the Qiantang, lost forever. The documentary *Jaws of the Dragon* made no reference to the first ride as there was no film evidence to show, but crew member Andy Long had taken some stills. Matthews concluded, 'I think the film company had some embarrassment not changing the film and the perception that I had only ridden the wave once and for only seconds came over in the film'.

It seemed as though this incredible attempt by Stuart Matthews inspired a new level of policing safety, and access to the water during the tidal bore became even more restricted. And for good reason. The bore was continuing to threaten spectators every single year. Just being close to it on the river bank was dangerous enough. Tide watchers had drowned regularly through the 1980s and 1990s and into the 2000s on big river bores after getting swept into the water. And, as we know, this Chinese love-hate affair with the *yin* and *yang* of the Qiantang spans three millennia.

I eventually concluded that getting permits would be impossible without any government contacts or official invites. Our only option was to first witness the bore as tourists, then try and ride it in secret, like the outlaw *nong chao er*. Perhaps it was an impossible dream, but the rebellious spirit of the Monkey King was burning bright inside me. But I knew we needed some expertise on modern-day bore riding. While Stuart Matthews was the global bore expert of the '80s and '90s, by the 2000s, Frenchman Antony Colas was the world's bore riding specialist. Colas cut his teeth studying and riding the Mascaret, that runs through southern France and Bordeaux. This is Europe's premier bore wave along with the Severn, gaining strength from big Atlantic tides. Colas went on to explore and map several other river bores around the planet. But Stuart Matthews had proven that the Qiantang was a unique challenge. It was the Silver Dragon, far bigger and much meaner than European bores, comparable only in scale and strength to the Pororoca in Brazil. The Silver Dragon and Pororoca were surely the Everest and K2 of river bores. While other bores rarely surpass two meters in height, the Silver Dragon can reach four or five, especially if a typhoon is churning away in the East China Sea.

It turned out that Colas had been researching the Qiantang for several years and was initiating his own project to ride it.

He knew all about the pioneering trip of Stuart Matthews, but nothing of the ancient *nong chao er*. He also knew that China is a strictly controlled Communist country and entering the river was illegal, unless, of course, the government gives you permission. Colas had attempted to get a permit to ride the bore, but he received no responses from the authorities. This was a perfect opportunity to join forces. The Silver Dragon lay waiting.

CHAPTER FOURTEEN

SHOOTING THE TIDE

Hangzhou in October 2007 was a far cry from the view that inspired Pan Lang and Zhou Mi's poetry and prose. It was a long way from the Song capital where emperors sipped *Long Jin* (dragon well) green tea grown in small manicured bushes overlooking the West Lake. But despite the heavily fortressed banks, the Qiantang River wave was still breaking during every pushing tide. And that's why I came here with photographer John Callahan, one day before the rest of the surf crew, hoping to witness the tidal breath of the delta. This is the famed 'Southern landscape' that I had read so much about whilst discovering the *nong chao er*. But the rumbling jade green wave painted in the Tang and Song poetry and sculptured in the Qiongzhu Temple back in Yunnan seemed to sing of a past that had been completely erased by 20th century industrial China.

Callahan and I climbed the ancient wooden steps of Hangzhou's most recognisable building, the 60 metres tall Liuhe (Six Harmonies) Pagoda, to get our first elevated view along the northern bank of the Qiantang. The Pagoda was first built in 970, destroyed in 1121, then reconstructed in 1165 during the Southern Song. It is one of the very few Song buildings surviving in the whole of China. Despite the lure, the view was far from attractive: thick factory smoke, chestnut coloured skies, steel-grey brackish river waters and the dark concrete vaults of the Qiantang Bridge built in the 1930s. The river looked defeated, exhausted. I scratched my head in disbelief. Exploring

Qiantang's muddy womb, looking for waves, already appeared doomed to failure.

"Flat and foggy," said Callahan with his trademark measured minimalism. The tidal bore wave was on its way, but bad light is a surf photographer's worst nightmare. The light was terrible. And Callahan doesn't do nostalgia. China is just another interesting place on Callahan's world map that engages with equal measure across the seven continents, five oceans and numerous seas. But I had been enthusiastically telling him all morning how generations of *nong chao er,* several Song emperors and Mao Zedong himself walked these very stairways of the Six Harmonies Pagoda checking the wave before us. Callahan nodded in agreement, then looked up, scrutinised the grey sky, then scowled in disapproval. I turned away from the river towards the park and the manicured cypresses of Full Moon Hill that offered a rare glimpse of the 'Jiangnan' (South of the River) region so celebrated in the art and literature of the Tang and Song. But turning back towards the river, the old environment of the *nong chao er* was radically different from the days of wave-riding spectacles at the Mid-Autumn Festival. Hangzhou now sits at the heart of an overwhelming coastal megalopolis that crawls like a concrete dragon from the ocean inland across three provinces.

Hangzhou itself hosts 8 million people, while nearby Shanghai (the largest city in China) hosts 22 million. The whole so-called 'Delta Urban Area' is twice the size of California, and still growing, home to 115 million across 100,000 square kilometres and 23 towns and cities, dwarfing any sense of nature - no trees, no beaches, no mountains in sight. Nature here, at least the version that the *nong chao er* would have cherished, was euthanised in development during the mid 20th century. The tsunami-like growth of this area was triggered by Chairman Mao's successor, Deng Xiaoping's and his pragmatic *gaige kaifang* 'open door' approach to the economy. 'I don't care whether the cat is black or white, as long as it catches mice', proclaimed Deng. The result was the highest economic growth rate in the world. Today the Chinese inhabit a reality that by its sheer scale (one-sixth of the globe) and economic potential, puts everyone else in the shade. To be Chinese is to belong to the oldest civilisation on earth, continuous for 25 centuries. Yet despite the suppression of history during Maoism, and lack of ancient buildings, you don't have to go far to find celebrations of China's rich traditions. In the adjacent Full Moon Hill Park there is a memorial to one of the most recited verses of Tang poetry, written by Hangzhou governor and Buddhist Bai Juyi (772-846) called 'Remembering Jiangnan (South of the River)':

yì jiāngnán   bái jū yì
忆江南 白居易

Remembering Jiangnan by Bai Juyi

jiāngnán hǎo   fēngjǐng jiù céng ān
江南好　风景旧曾谙

Jiangnan is good, Its scenery has long been known by all.

rì chū jiāng huā hóng shèng huǒ   chūn lái jiāng shuǐ lǜ rú lán
日出江花红胜火　春来江水绿如蓝

At sunrise, the river flowers burn bright red,
In spring, the river green turns blue.

néng bú yì jiāngnán
能不忆江南

How could one forget Jiangnan?

In another poem called 'Wave-beaten Shore', Bai Juyi, lamenting for a lover, writes, *'Asking if this tidal bore brings up the ocean's water, Is like asking if your feelings now still include my heart. I'd rather trust the tide than our feelings of regret. Missing you, I start to think the ocean is not so wide'.* The spirit of the tide, and it's poetic impact, was clearly still celebrated in Hangzhou. But instead of flowers as red as fire, an endless procession of yellow cranes, commercial compounds and factories now pierced the skyline of Xiaoshan district. The blue-green water had long gone. The river water was now dark brown. But yes, the wave still comes, roaming up the delta on the rising tide. And forecasting the river bore is precise to the very second of arrival.

Callahan was getting ready, lens in hand, to 'shoot the tide'. Poised at the top of the Pagoda I told him about the great folktale of 'shooting the tide' from the 'founding father' of Hangzhou, King Qian Liu (852-932) of the Wu. His kingdom flourished between the end of the Tang dynasty and the founding of the Song (907-60), during a period known as the Five Dynasties and Ten Kingdoms. The tidal bore was always a threat to farmland and homes along the river, particularly for the four days in a row during the largest tides twice a month. And it was extremely expensive to maintain and repair protective dykes and sea walls. The far longer and broader Yellow River was also known to be expensive to manage (thanks more to rainwater and flooding than tidal bores), coining the saying, 'gold it costs for the daily repair of the Yellow River, silver is needed for the Qian'. Whilst battling to build a sea wall, in an attempt to appease the raging tide of the Dragon God, King Qian Liu ordered 500 soldiers to shoot 3,000 bamboo arrows (decorated with bright feathers, painted red and tipped with newly fired metal) into the tide. After they had fired five rounds the tide turned away. King Qian Liu's 'sea wall' (塘 *tang*) was acknowledged when the river itself was named after him. The 錢江 Qian Jiang eventually became known as the 錢塘

江 Qiantang Jiang. Importantly, before King Qian Liu's soldiers shot the tide, he first made a sacrifice to Wu Zixu in the hope of placating the spirit of the tide. Remember Wu Zixu, whose corpse had been cast into the river, and his righteous anger against a cruel fate advising his Emperor about imminent war from the rival Yue, was believed to cause of the tidal tumult. It's important to recognise that at the time arrows fired to ward off the Dragon God were as important as the science and engineering in building the sea wall. Mythology and science went hand-in-hand in dynastic China.

But the tide was never tamed and dynastic chronicles are filled with tragic episodes of tide watching. Such tidal fatalities even have of a specific term: 潮患 *cháo huàn* or 'tidal vexation'. In reaction, rulers made annual sacrifices to appease the Dragon God. Notable *cháo huàn* incidents include 775 (during the Tang dynasty) when the combination of a large tide and a summer typhoon destroyed over 5,000 houses, killing hundreds. Similarly, in 1472, 1628 and 1770, hundreds of thousands of people lost their lives when the wave broke the embankment, submerging the adjacent fields for kilometres, triggering famine and poverty, and the latter event accelerating the fall of the Ming dynasty itself. Again, in 1926 130,000 people had to be evacuated when the wave engulfed the riverbed. And in 1997 the wave broke the river wall in 78 spots, submerging kilometres of farm land. In fact, from the 8th to the 20th century the river had inundated the banks over 230 times, mostly along the densely populated northern bank of Hangzhou.

Regardless of the danger, over 200,000 people per day still crowded these fortress-like banks during the Mid-Autumn Festival in September or early October, when the full moon amplifies the effects of the tide. They are all pulled by the same magnetic attraction to the energy of this monster - to feel it's power, measure it's force or get as close as possible in daredevil antics.

Imagine the reverence of the ancient tide players who rode its energy long before extreme sports were shared on media platforms around the planet. The show that enchanted poets and painters is now broadcasted live on national *CCTV*, reaching hundreds of millions. The entrance price to premier viewpoints (like the Six Harmonies Pagoda) during the Mid-Autumn Festival soars from 10 Yuan to 100 Yuan. But we were here one month after the Mid-Autumn Festival on a weekday in late October with a tide range of four meters (out of a possible nine), and it was fairly quiet with 'wave-watchers'.

"It should be here in 15 minutes," I said to Callahan while flipping the pages of the tide-charts, reminding him that the oldest tide charts in the world were made for this very river, back in 1056. "Maybe we should have been here... 800 hundred years ago," joked Callahan, still shell-shocked by how ugly the whole area had become, and finally now a bit nostalgic for the golden age of the *nong chao er* during the Song dynasty.

'You should have been here yesterday' is the cliché heard by surfers all around the world. It makes me feel red with rage because 'you missed it'. The line was popularised in Bruce Brown's pioneer surf travel film *The Endless Summer* (1966) where Californians Mike Hynson and Robert August travel on a three months long around the world trip in 'search of the perfect wave' through Senegal, Ghana, Nigeria, South Africa, Australia, New Zealand, Tahiti, Hawaii and California. In Australia they arrive just after a good swell. It's gone flat and local up-and-comers Nat Young and Rod Sumpter tease them with 'you should have been here yesterday'. From the relentless amount of research I had done in books and internet searches, I felt like I'd been back in old Hangzhou for the last two years. This only accentuated the feeling that we really had missed it.

"You're right Callahan, we should have been here 800 years ago. The river was way wider, river edge was more beach like, water was deeper and cleaner, and surf was better under the Song." I reached for my moleskin, pulled out an image, and passed it to Callahan. "Check this out." It was a reprint of a fan leaf titled 'Qiantang River Tide in Autumn', brushed around 1200 by Hangzhou painter Xia Gui (1195-1224), arguably the most talented landscape artist of the Southern Song. It depicts this same section of the river from a higher ground, and the same perspective described by Zhou Mi in 'Contemplating the Tide'.

On the left side of the leaf you can see the Six Harmonies Pagoda that we had just climbed standing proud. It is the only recognisable feature in the whole panorama. In front of it, the tidal wave cuts the scene in two. On the lower left side, plumes of menacing white foam rise up. The white frothy fangs give an angry character to the wave, rendered with short black calligraphic strokes. This section does not just surge, it rages forward, possibly depicting a barrelling wave for the first time in visual arts. This is the *yang*, assertive part of the painting, where everything, even individual pine needles and leafy plants, are precisely portrayed. The upper half offers still water, archetypal *yin*, with five fishermen working a small barge with the typical square sail. Four layers of low lying hills, completely invisible today, are rendered with soft shades of grey and dotted by vegetation.

"Look at that barrel," said Callahan, pointing at the leaf with his overgrown pinkie nail. "All the wave energy seems to focalise here on the north bank and break left. There's no foam on the south side." Due to a combination of river bed depth (bathymetry), wave refraction and flow orientation, the northern bank has always been hit the hardest by the tidal bore. A map printed in 1160 inside a local gazette called *The Lin'an Chronicles* also shows the wave focalising on the left side and the fortified northern bank. The whole town seemed to be built around (and against) the tide. The nearby sea wall first built by the Tang with sand, lime and boiled rice was further fortified to up to 20 meters in height under the Song, Ming and Qing dynasties, the exterior textured like fish scales, and known as 'The Great Wall on Water', where regular offerings and ceremonies were made to placate the raging waves. Building and maintaining this has been one of the largest engineering feats in Chinese history.

"How big do you think this wave was in Xia Gui's leaf?" asked Callahan, characteristically scratching his goatee. "If we use the trees and the pavilion as a reference, I'd say two, three meters." "Wow. The *nong chao er* had it pretty good!"

Callahan knew about my recent research, but I'd been pretty secretive about the full extent of the work. In the last year I had read countless poems, gazed at numerous paintings and translated reams of dynastic chronicles about this phenomenon. I couldn't wait to witness it, or 觀 *guān* 'contemplate' it as Song poets would say, with the lens of Callahan, one of the best surf photographers in the world. Callahan was a fitting match for a modern-day Song landscape painter. But what does surf photography have in common with Chinese landscape painting? Surf photography is all about action, and Callahan is an expert at capturing manoeuvres. But his specialism is framing these moments in the context of the place, where the surfer is insignificant relative to the majesty of the landscape. "Context is everything," says Callahan. He is a specialist in taking images of empty perfect waves, or a lone rider on one wave. They sum up the emotions behind surf exploration like nothing else.

夏圭 Xia Gui
錢塘秋潮圖 *qiantang qiuchao tu*
View of the Qiantang Bore in Autumn
Silk fan, 1200

臨安志 *linan zhi*, Lin'an Chronicles
浙江圖 *zhejiang tu*, Zhejiang Map
Wood-block print, 1256 - 1274

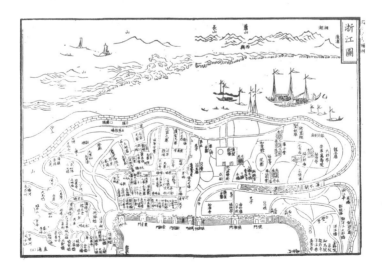

A highlight of editing *SurfNews* was working with Callahan's material, and his images (usually 'line-ups' of empty waves or lone riders) made many covers. Callahan, a great student of photography and graduate in Design from the College of Fine Arts, UCLA in Los Angeles, was inspired by the French philosopher Roland Barthes (1915-1980) and the power of photography explored in *Camera Lucida* (1980). Discussing the emotional impact of a photograph of his late mother, Barthes developed the twin concepts of *studium* and *punctum*. The *studium* is the geopolitical and cultural element of a photograph, described by Barthes as 'a kind of education (civility, politeness) that allows discovery of the operator'. The*punctum*is the personal element, jumping out at the viewer from the photograph, described by Barthes as 'that accident which pricks, bruises me' from an 'element which rises from the scene'. Callahan's composition is often divided into three vertical thirds, with the breaking wave only occupying one of the segments. This leaves plenty of room for multi-layered backdrops, crossed by unbroken swell lines. In Callahan's photos, water and land seem to feed off each other. In many ways, Xia Gui's leaf is a classic 'line-up shot'. In the Roland Barthes terms, the wave constitutes the *punctum* of the scene, but the background is the *studium* and thus leads the narration. The background puts the wave into context, conveying physical and social information about the area. Human beings are not necessarily part of Callahan nor Xia Gui's vision. They tend to constitute dark dots, or stylised silhouettes.

Through editing *SurfNews* I always felt a great attraction to line-up shots. They leave the reader/viewer entranced. In Chinese, 'reading' and 'viewing' are translatable with the same character, 看 *kàn*. As surfers we similarly 'read' the ocean before paddling out. Assessing the conditions, we might count the number of waves in a set, the time between sets of waves, check rip currents and absorb vital information. For me, line-up shots celebrate this moment of 'reading' and 'viewing' as one. Chinese art also reflects on this dichotomy. The word for landscape art, 山水 *shānshuǐ*, literally translates 'mountains and waters'. And painters like Xia Gui used the character 写 *xiě* (write) to describe their art, employing the tools of the scholar - brush and black ink - and focusing on five primary shades: heavy, light, thirsty, dry and white.

In the history of Western landscape painting, people have commonly been the subject, while the landscape is a backdrop. In Chinese landscape painting, human figures are often hidden away. The *studium* includes river and ocean waves and the foam and mist they generate when they collide with land. During the Song waves were extensively researched by Daoist painters. Ma Yuan's (1160-1225) 'Studies on Water' with its precise depictions of surging, spilling and plunging waves influenced not only Xia Gui, but generations of landscape artists to follow, including Li Guangxiu (sculptor of the the *luohan* of the Qiongzhu Temple in Yunnan) and Japanese woodblock print master Katsushika Hokusai (1760-1894) and his world famous 'The Great Wave off Kanagawa'. In all of these examples humans are only present to testify the magnitude of nature. Rich or poor, monks or fishermen, all play the same marginal role: insignificant and cloaked in fog, rowing upstream on a fragile barge, walking along a snowy ridge, or contemplating a passing wave from the banks of a river.

Such landscapes, often painted on long scrolls to depict tall mountains, are uplifting, literally. The reader/viewer travels around the scene, like wandering on foot. There's no main topic. The entire painting is not intended to reproduce what the eye sees, but to depict the essence of a place. The reader/viewer draws the narrative from the particular path taken through the artwork. And the scroll shape was dependent on context. In

1127 the northern Mongols conquered the capital Kaifeng and destroyed the imperial art academy burning over 6,000 masterpieces. The capital of the Southern Song moved to Hangzhou and the painting style changed with new strokes to render the flat, horizontal riverine landscape. Not surprisingly artists from Hangzhou, like Xia Gui, pushed Chinese landscape art to new levels, and the Qiantang became a dominant theme.

With Xia Gui's leaf print in hand, camera hanging around his neck, Callahan turned his eyes from the painting to the river, ready to shoot the tide as if now inspired by King Qian himself. "Here we go," he said, before placing his right eye on the viewer, trying to spot the wave to the east. "*Chao laile*" screamed one of the tourists. "The tide is coming." I couldn't see it, but there was an eerie sound. I thought of *Journey to the West* when the Monkey King transforms into a fly, lands on a blade of grass to wait beside the path and hears a rustling noise that he compares to the first audible sound of the tidal bore or '呼呼吸吸 *hū hū xī xī*, silk worms eating leaves'. The sound got louder. Then in the distance a thin white line appeared, spanning the width of the river, preceded by two speedboats of the local authorities, their engine noise drowned by the rising roar of the wave. Suddenly I noticed that the river was running out towards the ocean at an astonishing speed below us and several sand bags were getting dragged away from the banks in front of the Pagoda.

"Look at that. Water must be very shallow around there," noted Callahan as the whitewater gathered up and tumbled forward like an avalanche. The wave now carried a high-pitched noise, more like a landslide of rocks than the 'countless steel drums' reported in Pang Lang's poem. I thought again of *Journey to the West* where Pig and the Monkey King fight a demon living among the waves of Flowing Sand River where they heard the waves make a roar like collapsing mountains (波翻若岭 *bō fān ruò líng*) as a most hideous evil spirit emerged from the water. Then the sound dissipated as the line itself fragmented into three sections, alternatively showing white-water and open unbroken walls where the river bed deepened. As it came close to the bank it suddenly started peeling like an ocean wave in perfect cadence on a shallow, silty beach break. "That's Xia Gui's left there," I said to Callahan, "and look at that right just upfront here." We frantically moved to another view on the Pagoda, following the wave, east to west, mind-surfing it until it disappeared, leaving behind vicious dark whirlpools and a musky tang of stirred mud.

West of Xiaoshan district the Qiantang turns south, into what looks like of a vast gulf of river water. The tide had already travelled over 100 km, continued past the Six Harmonies Pagoda, exhaled its last breath and disappeared. We descended the steps, and met our driver. Comparing Callahan's digital images to Xia Gui's leaf, everything around had changed. But the left-hander section had remained intact.

We had three more big daylight tides to come. We had to collect the surf crew, spend a day researching entry and exit points, then attempt to ride the wave on the last two big tides of the lunar month.

CHAPTER FIFTEEN

A SURVEY OF THE SILVER DRAGON

After watching that first wave of the new spring tide from the Six Harmonies Pagoda in Hangzhou, Callahan and I travelled with our driver Mr Liu to Xiaoshan Airport to collect a mix of Italian and French surfers, then headed back into the city to our booked hotel. Distances in urban China are best described in hours of traffic rather than kilometres. Consequently 50 km took four hours. Finally, we made it to the Bore Watching Resort, a hotel advertised as 'the best spot for wave-watchers' with a look-out terrace over the river. It's built on a rocky headland, a rare geological feature along the muddy, flat, south side of the Qiantang. Like the Six Harmonies Pagoda, it is devoted to the practice of 'contemplating the tide', but with a postmodern twist. In the surrounding garden there's a prefabricated Song style pavilion, decorated with green foliage, but it's miniaturised, merely a plastic prop for tourists to pose in front of during the Mid-Autumn Festival, when the crowds arrive.

We checked in with a van-load of surfboards, expecting to meet Frenchman Antony Colas and his crew who had arrived a few days earlier. The lobby wall sports a massive painting depicting the oncoming wave, its head morphed into a dragon, storming past the area of Yanguan in Haining. 'Silver Dragon' is the perfect name for this ancient tide show that has now become a billionaire business. And even if tourism and mobility in general had been strongly ostracised during the peak of Maoist rule, 'contemplating the tide' never disappeared. And Mao himself was one of the biggest fans. In September 1957, when staying at the opulent Liu Villa on the West Lake, Mao visited the Qiantang to see the tidal bore and wrote a quatrain (four-line poem) in perfect Tang Dynasty style, to mark the occasion. Mao's 'Observing the Tide' (觀潮 *Guan Chao*), is still learned by heart in local schools. It's stencilled on the lobby wall:

qī jué guāncháo   *máo zédōng*
七絕 觀潮 - 毛泽东

Observing the Tide by Mao Zedong

qiān lǐ bō tāo gǔngǔnl ái   *xuě huā fē i xiàngd ià oyú tái*
千里波濤滾滾來　雪花飛向釣魚臺

Stretched out waves approach with a rumbling sound,
White foam like snowflakes covers the fishing docks.

rénshān fēn zàn zhènróng kuò   *tiě mǎ cōngróng shā dí hui*
人山紛讚陣容闊　鐵馬從容殺敵回

A multitude quietly admires the vast array,
Waves like iron clad horses returning from the battlefield.

Mao Zedong prided himself on being a strong swimmer, both in the pool (a must in any of his villas) and in rivers (he grew up swimming the Xiang River in his home province Hunan) and the ocean (spending his holidays on the Bohai Sea) and often opened his flamboyant campaigns with a symbolic show of water bravery. There are some great anecdotes written by his private doctor Li Zhishui in *Private Life of Chairman Mao*. In July 1955 Mao was spending a summer break in Beidaihe on the Bohai Sea, a popular escape from the searing summer heat in Beijing. There was a solid south swell and Mao planned a morning swim. But his bodyguards were worried for his safety and tried to stop him. Mao nevertheless jumped in, followed by a group of bodyguards. Mao's wife Jiang Qing and head bodyguard Wang Dongxing followed on the beach, while Liu Shaoqi, second in charge in the Maoist pyramid, was informed by telephone in Beijing. Mao's doctor and two soldiers rowed out into the surf on a small boat. But they struggled in the swell, and the doctor got seasick, while Mao had already body-surfed through the shore-break and returned to the beach. Mao saw these efforts to protect his safety as an infringement on his freedom to play in the waves. He was furious and apparently shouted 'You bastard' to Wang Dongxing, 'You should know that I can swim under these conditions. But you not only tried to stop me, you tried to intimidate me by getting the other party leaders involved'. The episode had serious consequences. Wang Dongxing was never trusted again and consequently removed from his position.

The following summer back in Beidaihe, Mao continued to swim. He had a raft set up offshore where he could head to, sunbath, then swim back to shore. A number of sharks had been sighted, so the bodyguards bought a caught shark from the fishermen, placed it on the beach to deter Mao (which failed), and set up a net around the raft. But Mao still ventured outside of the nets to prove his courage.

Courage, of course, was an important symbol for Mao. He had sealed his status as a strong leader through the 1936 Long March - a military retreat of 9,000 km by the Red Army of the Communist Party through the gruelling terrain of western China into the remote northwest to escape the Nationalist Party. In the horrors of the Japanese invasion that followed in 1937, national resistance was born, and Communism grew in popularity. While the Nationalists and Communists formed the Liberation Front during World War Two, post war the Nationalists fled to Taiwan, and in 1949 Communist Party leader Chairman Mao proclaimed the establishment of the People's Republic of China. He was soon celebrated for his attention to health, education, and the social equality and the rights of women that was missing in dynastic China. Yet Mao took Marxist ideas of common ownership to the extreme through his own vision for Communism.

Mao's visit to the Qiantang was to officially launch the Great Leap Forward, an aggressive attempt to radically boost industrial output. Like a cult figure Mao governed absolute power with giant and spectacular building operations. But the forced agricultural collectivisation (where private farming was prohibited) happening at the same time proved a disaster. The failures inspired Mao to reassert his political and social strength in the Cultural Revolution between 1966 and 1976.

The symbolism behind swimming and taming waves was a constant in Mao's personality cult. At every public appearance 'the eternal leader' showed his people he was fit for rule and ready to push ahead, in his own words, 'against big waves and strong wind'. In a famously staged performance in 1967, now aged 73, while launching the Cultural Revolution, Mao entered the Yangtze River in Wuhan, the biggest and most fierce of all Chinese rivers. He loved being carried by the current feeling it's raw and natural power. He floated for two hours and emerged 10 km downstream, apparently 'reborn' in the eyes of the audience, still the 'Great Helmsman', ready to carry the country forward. Mao governed China the way he swam, believing in dangerous, risky policies.

The hotel lobby, with its festooned walls, was reminiscent of those heady days of Maoism. It is a massive space that can host hundreds. But in October it was empty, except for a bored clerk in a pale uniform sitting at the reception desk. We headed towards him to check-in. But the moment he eyed up the surfboards he got on the phone, looking concerned. "There are *laowai* here with boards," said the receptionist to whoever was at the other end of the line, surely expecting that none of us would be able to understand Chinese. *Laowai* is the word for 'foreigner'. Its literal translation is 'old friend from abroad', although it has a more derogatory meaning as someone from the outside, who most likely 'eats raw meat and drinks cold water'. The receptionist hung up and collected our passports suspiciously, checked our tourism visas, begrudgingly forced a smile and said, "Welcome. Here are your room keys," in broken English. After I replied in Mandarin he then turned to me to continue (in Mandarin), "Please take the lift to the fourth floor and turn right. I'll return your passports tomorrow." This was unusual for a Chinese hotel, where documents are rarely kept for longer than a few minutes. "He's surely reporting us to the authorities," I concluded as we loaded boards and bodies into the elevator.

We caught up with Antony Colas and his crew and ate at a smoky noodle bar across the road. Colas confirmed that the authorities were already suspicious of them as they spent the last two days scouting around the river with their surfboards and looking for a jet ski to hire. Callahan was furious that they might have blown our chances to ride the bore by raising too much attention too early. Nevertheless, we made plans and met up for breakfast early the following morning at a stall just aside a bustling street market run by local fishermen. The famed *nong chao er* could be the ancestors of these fishermen, and I knew I'd need to start talking to them. But right now the agenda was to survey the next tide.

We crammed into the hired van with our driver Mr Liu and headed east, downstream. With three thousand years of 'contemplating the tide', tide charts not only dictate the exact timing, but maps also show the shape that the wave will assume at the major viewing points. Famed for generations as one of China's 'remarkable spectacles' (奇觀 *qíguān*), the various local descriptions of the tides include 'criss-crossed tides' (交叉潮 *jiāochā cháo*), 'single-line tides' (一線潮 *yīxiàn cháo*), 'returning tides' (回頭潮 *húi tóu cháo)*, 'midnight tides' (半夜潮 *bànyè cháo)*and 'T-tides' (丁字潮 *dīngzì cháo*).

The tide chart said that the wave would first arrive at 11.00 am in the area of Ganpu, almost 50 km from the hotel. We followed the northern bank, witnessing the river widening and the landscape turning from urban to industrial, then to rural. We positioned ourselves on the elevated banks. In celebration of King Qian Liu's 500 soldiers who shot the tide with 3,000 arrows, two of the roads here are named 'The Horizontal Arrow Lane-way (橫箭道巷 *Héng Jiàn Dàoxiàng)*' and 'The Vertical Arrow Lane-way (直箭道巷 *Zhì Jiàn Dàoxiàng)*'. From here the Qiantang appeared wide and serenely still. But then, just before 11.00 am I noticed a vitality to the ripples. Small, tide-induced waves started to hit each other throwing miniaturised spray as if a submerged dragon was awakening and gently shaking its scales under the surface. The whole body of water was soon vibrating. The energy became tangible, electric even. Then it suddenly stopped, and the river was stretched flat by the oncoming surge.

The wave appeared right on time. In its infancy, here at the river-mouth it was made of two separate lines, one coming from the east, the other from the south. The twin bores had not started to white cap yet. They just advanced like the 'silver lines' described by Zhou Mi, oxidising into to a darker colour as their heads met. They moved slowly as if river curtains were lifting for the show to begin. Wave-watchers call this the 'number ten wave' from the character 十 *shí* 'ten' formed by the intersection of the two perpendicular lines. This lasted only a few minutes, then dissipated by hitting the northern bank at the first meander, producing a tall wall of foam that marked the beginning of the long 'single line phase'.

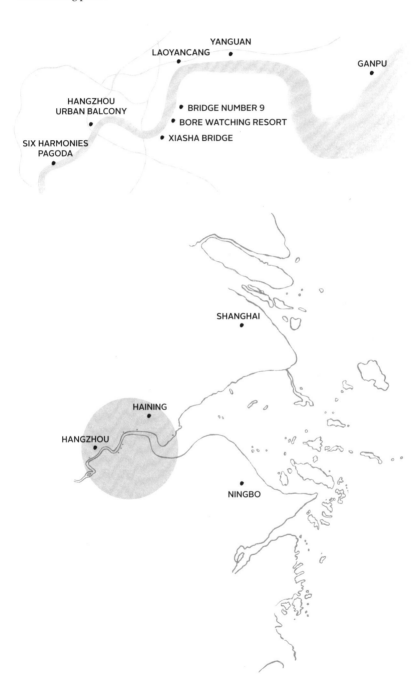

YANGUAN

LAOYANCANG

GANPU

HANGZHOU
URBAN BALCONY

BRIDGE NUMBER 9

BORE WATCHING RESORT

SIX HARMONIES
PAGODA

XIASHA BRIDGE

SHANGHAI

HAINING

HANGZHOU

NINGBO

We ran back to the van and started following the bore while it moved upstream, overtaking it, then stopping to map its interaction with the bathymetry and the various human constructions it encountered. Sound, then view, and finally smell mixed together at each stop. The narrower the river, the taller the bore became. The taller the bore, the louder it became. The louder it became, the stronger the smell of stirred mud. In some places it was pungent, almost nauseating. We followed the bore across the scenic spots of Yanguan, where a famous temple of the Dragon God was built in the 17th century. The banks here are also dotted by solid bronze statues of water buffalos and freshwater turtles, three metres in length. They placate the fury of the tide, but bring dubious results as a few of them have been overturned by the bore, and thrown down their pedestals.

The river is perfectly linear in this section, a clear sign of human intervention. Consequently, the tidal bore takes the shape of a long line of white water, spanning the entire river width. "Close out," we all agreed, as the wave broke all at once, not 'peeling off' in one particular direction. While this doesn't offer any value for surfers, local wave-watchers and travelling tide-voyeurs see this section as the perfect incarnation of the spirit of Wu Zixu, or the God of the Tide himself, riding a dragon, blowing steam from the nostrils as he rushes upriver.

The furious white-water hit buildings, producing deep thundering claps and throwing foam an incredible 20 metres into the air. I could only imagine the magnified intensity of the bigger bore wave during the Mid-Autumn Festival in one month. As if toying with the sometimes fatal danger, the local municipality had cemented fake boats on top of protruding jetties to increase the spectacle. Around these we spotted a few potentially surfable sections, mainly aside piers and loading stations. But without a permit, jet ski or a speed boat, anyone attempting to ride these would most in the shallow mud banks that regularly reared up unexpectedly, and then swallowed whole by the ever-advancing dragon.

The wave then took a spectacular turn further inland where it reached the first 90-degree elbow at Laoyancang, Haining district. This is a 'must see' among wave-watchers. Here the procession of mopeds and cars stopped, and everyone scrambled to find an elevated view point. The bend is a result of construction works completed in 1980. It appears like a vast amphitheatre, 30 metres tall. The dragon hit it head on, with unimaginable fury, its head climbing nearly halfway up the structure, sending out a deep roar. This thundering sound is not the only consequence of the titanic clash. The whole structure shakes as if a giant ocean swell is striking the coast.

That sensation of collapsing mountains described by Zhou Mi could definitely be felt here. I had witnessed this before while watching huge surf explode close to shore in Australia. This is most spectacular at Pipeline, on the North Shore of Oahu, Hawaii, possibly the most intense and dangerous close-to-shore tubing wave in the world. But here at the bend in Laoyancang the sound of collapsing mountains seemed to happen in slow motion, and lasted minutes. It was a terrifying experience, and, of course, we were not the first to think this. There is a legendary episode related to this tide-induced earthquake. With his court chased by the invading Mongols, Emperor Gaozong (1107-1187) lead his army from Kaifeng, the northern capital, to Hangzhou to establish the Southern Song. On his first night in the new palace, located not far from the Qiantang, he suddenly woke up in fear, thinking that the invincible cavalry of the Jurcheng Mongols had arrived to siege the city. The noise of the passing wave 'as loud as ten thousand galloping horses' reminded him of his recent military defeats.

The Silver Dragon turned on itself here, the reflux from the impact rushing back towards the ocean, producing several ominous backwash waves that broke against the natural flow. "龙回头 *Lóng huí tóu* (It's the dragon is turning its head)," shouted the locals with excitement. This is where the *BBC* and *National Geographic* film crew with Stuart Matthews operated in 1988. The footage shows a red inflatable zodiac frantically running away from the bore, everyone clearly terrified by the monster.

The elbow of Laoyancang also marks the beginning of the best surfing sections. After the brutal clash the wave loses some of its chaotic fury and opens up into the rideable 'wall of jade' described by Zhou Mi. There is approximately 40 km from here to the Six Harmonies Pagoda, with the river leaving Haining municipality, entering Hangzhou territory, and meandering four more times.

Just past the imposing reinforced concrete pillars of Bridge Number Nine, the bore energy compressed, wave size rose, and the unsurfable wall of 'closed-out' white-water that had escorted us for almost one hour turned into a completely different surf-scape. First, we noted a massive left, forming just past the bridge and marching slowly towards the south wall, only one kilometre upstream from the Bore Watching Resort. It remained active for about one kilometre, morphing again into a long line of whitewater. A few minutes inland the foamy line disappeared into deep water, then rose up again just past the Xiasha Bridge, forming a perfect procession of three parallel right handers.

"This is possibly the longest rideable wave we have ever seen," exclaimed Callahan. This river bore phenomenon is called 'whelping', where parallel lines are broken up into peeling waves. Our crew hooted with joy and fear at the view, filled with both enchantment at the length of the ride, and terror at the absence of safe entry and exit points. While the Haining area offered a few easy to access mud banks that we could safely climb, getting to the river here in the Hangzhou municipality was blocked by docks, loading harbours and massive concrete constructions. This was the front-line in the historical battle between human settlement and natural floods that started during the Tang dynasty and was still raging.

But geographical hazards were only half the battle. Police were ubiquitous. They had speed boats motoring ahead of the wave and check-points in place at regular intervals. Add to this the multi-tude of plain-clothes informers willing to report any anomaly to the authorities via mobile phones, and our chances of riding the bore without getting caught were close to impossible. Some plain-clothes informers perhaps had already followed us during our in-spection of the bore and knew exactly what we were thinking. The bore continued to lure us with perfect sections, all the way to the Six Harmonies Pagoda, where the dragon finally disappeared.

We spent the afternoon reviewing our research and met for breakfast the next morning, aiming to ride the bore. But I knew that the key to success was talking to the local fishermen. And I had a plan. At the riverside near the hotel a small flotilla of fishing vessels rested peacefully. Green nets hung at their sides like the wings of cormorants drying in the easterly breeze. These flat-bot-tomed boats employed a simple technique: they anchored in a deep channel and dropped their nets before the night tide. At dawn they collected the catch and transferred it on slim wooden skiffs to the market. This technique was a perfect example of Daoist 'non-ac-tion'. They simply let the river do the hard work and deliver fish to their nets. Even if modernisation had transformed the entire area, turning the water from 'jade-green' to 'mud-brown', these fisher-men still carved a traditional existence in tune with the Qiantang.

The skiff this crew used to get ashore was interesting. It had a flat keel with sharp low rails and an elongated shape that surfers would recognise as 'gunny' ('pointy' at both ends), designed for 'big waves'. They propelled it with a two-stroke engine and used a long pole, often painted red at the top, when docking or manoeuvring over very shallow water. Their livelihood depended on this alteration between deep and shallow, high and low tide. That simple pole empirically linked them with the *Qi* of the Qiantang, giving them an instant report of what goes on above and below the river water. The deep channels they fished changed position every season, morphing in shape. Even local authorities equipped with modern bathymetry scanners had trouble keeping track of their mutations. A poem from Qing dynasty painter Zheng Xie (1693-1765) celebrated the fishermen's skills and their identifiable poles:

nòngcháo qǔ zhèng xiè
弄潮曲 - 鄭 燮

Playing with the Tide by Zheng Xie

qiántáng xiǎo ér xué nòngcháo
錢 塘 小 兒 學 弄 潮

On the Qiantang boys learn how to deal with the tide from a tender age,

yìnggāocháng jǐn à fù shāo
硬 篙 長 楫 捺 復 捎

Grown as tough as their punting pole,
they push and push with their oar.

duòlóu yī rén rú zhùtiě
舵 樓 一 人 如 鑄 鐵

On the helm deck alone, as hard as cast iron,

sǐ huīmiàn sèjīng bù yáo
死 灰 面 色 睛 不 搖

They look ahead, with a cold stare on their face.

There is no doubt that 'the brave watermen from Wu' described by Zhou Mi remained part of the cultural fabric of the Qiantang. I knew that the success of our surf attempts depended on the local knowledge of these fishermen. Without information about the changing bathymetry there was no way for us to know where to safely enter and exit the river. Also, they could help us dodge the authorities. I finished a breakfast of noodle soup and approached the fishing community in the nearby market.

Carp, the main item sold at the market, grow up to one metre long here, thriving in brackish water, and known locally as 胖头鱼 *pàngtóuyú* 'bighead fish'. They snapped their tails inside multi-coloured plastic baskets filled with yellowish water. *Aristichthys nobilis* (the Latin and scientific name for bighead carp) is in fact the prevalent species of this entire river. They have human-like eyes and have been regularly referenced in poetry and art, often associated with the tidal bore. And recall, the craft ridden by the *nong chao er* in the Qiongzhu Temple in Yunnan are carp. There was only one part of the historical literature (from Zhou Mi) that actually described 'drifting wood' being ridden. But references to riding on 'fish', or more specifically *pangtouyu,* were widespread. Everything was linking up, and knowing the fisherman would be suspicious of foreigners, I used my interest in the carp as a way to break the ice.

"Big headed carp. Don't they taste like mud?" I asked a slim, middle aged and weather-faced fish-stall owner in my best Mandarin. He was wearing a greasy green shirt and mud stained khaki trousers. His stall, on the outskirts of the market, seemed perfect for a discrete conversation. "Look at my treasures," he replied, pointing at two teenage boys, teasing the family's scruffy dog with a bamboo stick. "They all grew up on these bigheads. The meat is fat and tasty. No mud flavours. It sells for three times this price in restaurants downtown. Want to buy one?" "And how do you cook it?" "Just soak it in vinegar and ginger, and boil it."

Ice now broken, the fisherman offered me his callous hand and a cigarette. I accepted. It's hard, indeed impolite, to resist nicotine in China, and this is tough for health-conscious surfers. A saying goes: 'A smoke after dinner will make you live longer than an immortal saint'. The fisherman introduced himself as Mr Wu. His surname alone identified him as a local and inspired me to continue.

"Wu... an original *nong chao er*?" I said. Mr Wu coughed out a cloud of smoke, then planted his eyes into mine. "How does a foreign friend know about this old story?" I quickly pulled out my moleskin and quoted Pan Lang's poem, my mantra for the last two years, "The children of the tide go towards the head of the wave and stand up. They hold a red flag that never gets wet." Mr Wu listened with a knowing smile, looked at me in amazement, then lowered his eyes. "Those times are long gone," he said, now reflective. "The river has changed too much for those red flags," his tone now sad. "What do you mean by that?" I asked. "Red flags are everywhere in China." "When I was their age," he said, pointing towards his kids, "all sorts of oceanic fish would end up in our nets. Mud crabs, snappers, even sharks sometimes. But after all the development and the dredging, the channels became muddy and shallow. The water is fresh now, even at high tide. And we have turned from open water fishermen to riverside rats."

I knew from my research that the environment in this area had changed drastically from Mr Wu's teenage years to today. Most of the surrounding concrete embankments were developed through the mid to late 20th century when large-scale government operations gradually reduced the river width from 20 to 1.5 km. The first photographic evidence of this area, collected by the Zhejiang Institute of Hydraulics and Estuaries, is dated October 1892. It was taken from Haining, on the north bank, looking towards the Bore Watching Resort. The south bank is so far away it is almost invisible. Successive images of the tidal bore, reported in western periodicals such as the Illustrated London News in December 1910, confirm the original 'oceanic temper' of the area, with vast sandy bays, small coves and gulfs. The whole environment looked more coastal than riverine back then.

"And what about the wave? Did you guys ride it like the *nong chao er*?" Mr Wu looked around, checking if anyone was listening. Most of their trade happens at dawn. It was 8.00 am and the market was now nearly empty. "The tide's head was much taller. So tall it climbed all the way to the top of the mud bank. My dad taught us to tread waves on a wood plank, riding on our bellies. He used to say a long time ago they rode standing and had festivals and competitions. But it was only some families that did it, and those skills were lost and the practice was banned many times. But the authorities were not always watching, and some that did would tolerate the playing, so we used to grab a wood plank and slide on our bellies for fun, jumping in front of the wave from the shallows. It was underground and made us feel alive. Only a few of us did it. But the river changed too much. These concrete walls killed all the fun. Some got trapped while treading waves, drowning of a terrible death. Then the authorities would not tolerate it. The *nong chao er* died out a long time ago."

He looked at me quizzically. "But why are you asking all of this? Are you guys those foreigners?" "What foreigners?" "Everyone is talking about it. A group of *laowai* is in town with boards to tame the tide's head." I proudly admitted, "Yes that's us. We are *nong chao er,* like you. We flew over from Europe for this." He laughed nervously. "You should have been here 30 years ago! Playing was tolerated until the 1980s. Then they shut us down after too many accidents. It all became illegal. Chasing the wave is illegal. Dying is illegal. You'll get in trouble." I was going to ask Mr Wu if he remembered the bore-riding heroics of Stuart Matthews, but a white commercial van pulled up in the nearby esplanade, and his attention turned. It was a buyer from town. Mr Wu walked across to the driver, negotiated a price, then started to load fish in the refrigerated truck.

Callahan and the whole team now arrived at the market. Mr Wu came back again and checked them out, then turned to me, speaking quietly and directly. "I know one place where you can ride in secret. There's a construction plant two kilometres east from here on the south bank. They employ many foreigners. The guards are used to *laowai* in the property and their boss has lunch at 12 every day. Show up at five past 12 and tell them you are from the training centre. If they open the gates, you'll be safe. Just drive along the lower path so they don't see you. There's a jetty. The wave will hit at 12:30. The banks are shallow for three kilometres along that side, too shallow for the police boats. Fishermen don't operate in that area. Stick to the south shore where you can tread waves. That's a place we used to play. Good luck."

I thanked Mr Wu profusely, grabbed a few 100 yuan bills and tried to slide them inside his pocket. But he refused vigorously, "*Nong chao er* have always been rebels. May the Dragon King be with you," he said, then disappeared towards his boat.

Bore watching crowd near
the Six Harmonies Pagoda
October 2015

CHAPTER SIXTEEN

THE QIANTANG JIANG SHOOT-OUT

We decided to load our boards into the van in the middle of the night to avoid surveillance, used the fire escape stairs, then parked close to the market, far from the hotel property, ready for the mission incognito. Morning welcomed us with a thick fog, swallowing the river whole: a blessing if your daily plan includes hiding from police boats and the omnipresent cameras, a curse if you plan to photograph (or 'shoot the tide' as Callahan joked). Everything - bridges, boats, buildings - had been suffocated by the mist. Then the river started to glow, as if warmed from below. The silhouette of Mr Wu's fishing boat emerged on the still water like an ink painting from the Song.

The wave was forecast to hit at around 12:30, so I spent the morning sitting on Callahan's veranda, eating garlic flavoured pumpkin seeds and rehearsing our plan on Google Earth. I was nervous, my gut clenching when we walked through the lobby, past the suspicious clerk, sneaking out like thieves, mingling with a small crowd of tourists arriving to 'contemplate the tide' in what would be the biggest day of the month. They were heading west to the scenic spots of Yanguan and the Six Harmonies Pagoda, or to the Urban Balcony in Central Hangzhou where the show gathers the biggest crowd. We headed east, against the stream, towards what in dynastic chronicles was called the Ocean Gate.

The fog had now lifted, although it was still a smoggy, grey day. The road east was nearly empty, except for half a dozen women and men busy collecting bottles, cans and other food containers scattered along the edges. Faces shrouded in scarfs and breathing masks, they gathered leftovers while their partners waited for them aside three-wheeled 50cc vehicles with massive nylon bags fastened to the rusty trunk to carry the findings. China is both the biggest producer and the most active recycler of plastic on the planet. Scrap peddlers, mostly coming from the poorer countryside, inhabit the low end of the Chinese dream. They are the bottom of the national production chain, but still they smiled and waved a warm 'hello', the only English word they knew, as we passed by. Marginalised but still dignified, I thought of how we looked in comparison. Chinese nationalists might call us 'western devils', apparently 'rich enough' to waste time breaking the law. And in the Communist mantra, risking your life through extreme sports in search of personal thrill is surely an insult to collectivism: your work, your deeds, even your most private secrets are part of a wider scheme, a national identity and common goal. Taking chance in an unnecessary dangerous activity is the most futile and egotistical of crimes. 'Isn't surfing too dangerous?' was the concerned advice of most of the people I met while scouting unridden waves in Fujian, Guangdong and Zhejiang during past trips. Beaches all over China are often closed during the best typhoon swells due to the danger of the water. Ironically, extreme swimming Mao would have appreciated the thrill of surfing more than most. But the turbulent relationship between wave riders and the authorities has a very long history here, from governor Cai Xiang's first ban in 1065, to subsequent bans following the great displays described by Zhou Mi at the Mid-Autumn Festival.

I could not empty my mind of the historical high points for the *nong chao er* as we drove in silence, passing a dozen signs forbidding any water activity during the tidal surge. Would the *nong chao er* ever return?

It took 20 minutes to get from the hotel to the plant Mr Wu
had suggested. The compound was surrounded by tall barbed
wire, but its entrance was guarded by one man, hiding inside
a small watch tower and manning a simple iron bar. He nonchalantly rose his eye. "干嘛 *Gān ma?* (What's up?)" he asked.
"培训中心 *Péixùn zhōngxīn* (Training centre)," said our driver,
Mr Liu, as planned. As if by magic the bar lifted, and the guard
turned his eyes back to his mobile screen. We were in.

We took a left turn and followed a muddy track all the way to
the dock, a grey pile of concrete blocks jutting into the river for
about 50 meters. We parked behind a wall, out of sight from the
plant, and offloaded our gear. The team was electrified. Undeterred by the possible consequences - such as arrest, deportation
and denial of future visas - they waxed their boards and got into
their wetsuits. As the only Mandarin speaker in the crew, I resigned myself to the fact I'd need to keep a watchful eye on-land,
and let the pro surfers ride the wave. "We'll need to be ready for
a quick escape," said Callahan, as he opened his Manfrotto tripod
next to the van.

Just as I was about to answer, the sound of an approaching
motorbike caught my attention. A man dressed in a suit and jacket appeared on a sparkling new scooter. He looked concerned,
clearly dispatched by someone more senior, and worried about
being held responsible for the outcome. He went straight to Mr
Liu and showed him an identification card. "He must be an informer in plain clothes," I whispered to Callahan.

"What's going on here?" the informer asked, looking at the
surfers, now suited, boards under arm. "It's illegal to go into the
river without a permit. Tell them to leave the water's edge," he
added, and turned to Mr Liu demanding, "Show me your ID." Mr
Liu stood speechless. The informer started to yell at Mr Liu.

In a heated moment, ignorance can be bliss, so I pretended I did not understand Mandarin. Plan A was to let Mr Liu deal with it. After all, Mr Liu had proven to be completely onboard with our plans so far. Importantly, he was not a local driver, and Zhejiang police were not allowed to confiscate licenses from other provinces. This was exactly why we hired Mr Liu. But after being yelled at by the informer, Mr Liu now looked at me seriously concerned, and plan B was imminent.

"This guy might be from the central government, way above provincial administration," said Callahan, noting his expensive wrist watch and leather jacket. "Why are you helping them?" the informer continued to interrogate Mr Liu, "You will be held responsible for this."

I felt an irresistible urge to intervene and activate plan B, then turned to the river to see the silver line appear. The surfers were ready. "It's coming, let's rock and roll," yelled Callahan to the crew, urging them to get into the river. They moved like lightning. The informer ran to try and stop them. But they ran faster along the jetty and dived in like they were entering the ocean, only to realise that the water was only knee deep, too shallow to even paddle. They started wading towards the centre of the river, belly deep in mud, then sat on their boards, quickly drifting east, ready for the bore. Meanwhile our persecutor reached the end of the jetty, screaming his lungs out, first at the surfers in the water, then on his mobile phone, then at us. The next minute felt like an eternity while waiting for two imminent arrivals: the wave and the police. They arrived simultaneously, but this time not to 'the sound of countless steel drums' but with sirens blasting from the car roof.

The wave was far from impressive. A head-high wall of grey water crumbled in front of the surfers, ready to catapult them up stream. The informer ran away from the jetty seconds before the impact washed across the entire structure.

"Shitty closeout section," murmured Callahan while his Canon fired at maximum speed. "No media will ever buy this crap." The riders stood up and quickly disappeared. Callahan only had a few seconds to document the apex of a trip that took months to plan. Without following ahead of the riders on jet ski it was near impossible to shoot the bore. Callahan unmounted his camera and closed his tripod in frustration, concluding, "Ocean waves, not river waves, are my forte."

Two cars with government plates were now parked right in front and behind our van, blocking any escape route. Mr Liu, Callahan and I were the only ones left. Four policemen walked towards us. A small crowd of personnel from the plant also gathered. "I think it's time to speak up," urged Callahan, who seemed to be cooler than ever in the heat of the moment, and lit up a cigarette, offering a smoke to the policemen; none of them accepted.

I introduced myself to the officials. "Distinguished leaders," I started, nervously, their eyes now mesmerised, shocked I could speak Mandarin. I bowed respectfully with my hands clasped on my forehead, then continued. "On behalf of my sporting team I apologise for causing trouble. We are professional *nong chao er* and you can be reassured about our safety. We know what we are doing." "Safety is only one of our concerns," exclaimed a fiery young officer, eyes disappeared under his oversized military hat. "You trespassed private property, entered the river without a permit, and took pictures in a sensitive area. Didn't you see the English signs? Give us your passports, now." "I would surely do so, Comrade, but all our passports are at the Bore Watching Resort." I handed him the hotel business card. "Can we meet there in the afternoon? We now need to follow our team members and retrieve them."

I turned back to the river and in the distance saw three of the crew already left behind by the wave. It was Frenchmen Erwan Simon and Rico Baile, and Italian Francesco Palattella, who used small shortboards and had lost the wave at the first weakening of the surge, a few hundred meters from the starting point. They were trying to reach the shore, negotiating the turbulence and whirlpools behind the tide.

The policemen agreed to the plan, and moved away the blockade. We jumped in the van (followed by the police), picked up the first three surfers, and kept driving along the bank chasing the rest of the team. Frenchmen Antony Colas and Xavier Leroy were the next to lose the wave. They hit a mud bank and stopped abruptly, as if they had thrown anchor. They scrambled to the bank aiming to run alongside the wave and jump back in ahead of it, and ride again. This was a technique commonly used with other, slower, bores like the Mascaret in France and the Severn in the UK. And they were not alone. A local man in a grey vest, shaved head and bare feet, with a bag in his hand, ran alongside them. He looked half Buddhist monk, half fisherman and appeared in complete unity with the wave. Despite the mud, Colas and Leroy got ahead of the wave, jumped in again, but quickly lost the surge.

They ran along the bank once more, but the bore got the better of them, and they finally gave up and made it to shore, stained in mud and stinking like sewer rats. Meanwhile, the local guy just kept running at the same pace of the wave, perfectly familiar with every bank of mud, each rock and all the hostile and spiky vegetation. He stopped, picked up an egret that had been stunned by the tide, threw it into his bag, then sprinted on, disappearing like a ghost into the mist, together with the wave. It was surreal to say the least.

Frenchman Patrick Audoy and Brazilian Eduardo Bage were still going strong, heading north towards the opposite bank at speed, riding a 10'0" stand-up-paddle (SUP) board and 9'6" longboard respectively. Outside of the plant's property most of the roads and bridges were now blocked in the same cheerful chaos of wave-watchers once described by Zhou Mi. Food stalls sold candied rose-hips and steamed buns at several times the regular price. Following the outlaw surfers through the crowds by van would be impossible, even for the police. We were forced to leave the last two riders to their destiny and head back to the hotel.

By the time we regrouped in the lobby two hours later our passports were already orderly displayed on a table in front of a few empty chairs and cups of cheap green tea. In China when the police ask you to come and talk, they literally say, 'You must come over for a cup of tea' usually inferring that they have something quite 'bitter' to tell you. The officials sat down, sipped tea, and started filling out printed forms in ominous silence. I could see the words '禁止 *jìnzhǐ* (Forbidden)' written across the papers. I was now in a state of panic, expecting to be handcuffed and escorted to the police station for further interrogation.

We sat down on the chairs, eyes at the floor. After a few minutes of silence I was handed a pile of forms. "Sign these," demanded one of the officers. I looked at the papers for a few seconds, then looked up at the officer. "Excuse me for my poor Mandarin, but I don't understand what is written here. It would take me hours to translate this. But it surely says we are guilty of disrespecting the rules of the People's Republic of China. I cannot deny that. We just wanted to ride the best and strongest tide on the planet, like local fishermen and the *nong chao er* have done for thousands of years."

I pulled out a few copies of *SurfNews* magazine from my back-pack that documented our same crew during past exploration trips. One copy contained an article on the Pororoca in Brazil, the raging river bore travelling for 800 km up the Amazon and named after the indigenous Tupi language, combining a translation of the words 'great roar' and *'poroc-poroc'* which means 'to destroy everything'. It had been surfed since the late 1990s and there was now an annual bore-riding event. In 2005 Brazilian Sergio Laus achieved a record-breaking ride of 10.1 km lasting 33 minutes. He beat the 1996 record from the River Severn held by Dave Lawson of 9.6 km.

The head officer inspected the magazines, paying particular attention to the Pororoca feature, then looked up. "Fishermen and wave-watchers have died by the thousands in the past trying to play with the tide like you did. Some have died simply getting too close to it. What you have done constitutes a negative example for the multitude of bystanders that witnessed your bravado and may want to repeat it. We have recorded your passports and submitted your case to the immigration authorities in Beijing. We are not going to detain you here in Hangzhou, but you have 24 hours to leave."

We signed the papers. Our passports were given back. Not one page was stamped. The trial was over. The police left.

We regrouped when Patrick Audoy and Eduardo Bage arrived in a taxi, their massive boards loosely fastened on the roof. Their GPS device said that they rode the bore for 70 minutes and 17 km. They had unofficially smashed the world record for the longest ride. They had miraculously managed to 'shoot' five bridges, traversing the river several times, avoiding the jaws of the dragon by riding erect. When they got out of the river, police tried to interrogate them, but the language barrier (neither of them speak a word of Mandarin) played to their advantage, and after several unfruitful attempts, the police let them go, and the surfers found a willing taxi driver to bring them back to the Bore Watching Resort.

While this wasn't the largest tide of the year (when the bore would be bigger and more spectacular) their account of the ride revealed how the bore constantly changed shape over countless sand banks and deep-water channels. At times it almost disappeared, with steepness going under 20 degrees. Then it rose up suddenly, throwing a gaping but short-lived barrel, like the one depicted by Xia Gui. Such characteristics made it surfable only with their high buoyancy equipment. Shortboards or bellyboards would have lost speed and sunk during the many flat areas along the bore's path. Using a jet ski to pick up the surfers and reposition them in front of the wave would have helped tremendously, especially for the shortboarders, but this wasn't available for us, nor for the riders of the Song dynasty.

Patrick, riding the SUP with a paddle, proved to have the most functional board for length of ride. He explained how he not only used his paddle to propel his SUP during slow sections, he also used it to find his balance through turbulence and to punt in mud, the same way Mr Wu propelled his skiff from the fishing boat to the market through the shallows. The use of a pole for balance has a solid foundation in Chinese river-culture. A long pole is similarly used by the boatmen of the Yulong and Li rivers in Guangxi province to propel and balance on slim bamboo rafts during their traditional cormorant-fishing sessions. I had travelled with Callahan before to Yangshuo, where we worked on a travel magazine article documenting the Li and Yulong rivers. Watching the fishermen use bamboo rafts as stand-up paddle boards was astonishing. They could literally jump down rapids and small waterfalls and ride stationary waves produced by the fast current. And all this while carrying their fishing gear, a few tourists or a flock of cormorants trained to catch fish. The same tactic is also employed to row and find balance by the watermen of Guizhou province while riding erect on a single bamboo log. This technique called '独竹漂 *dú zhú piāo* (single bamboo drift)' now declared a UNESCO world heritage, is also typical on the Chishui river, a tributary of the Yangtze in Yunnan province, and was used to transport precious logs of the lucrative *nan* variety from the production areas to the markets. Even Monkey King speaks of a bamboo pole: when, in chapter one, he decides to leave his kingdom in the mountains and go searching for the Buddha, the immortals and the sages (the only creatures that don't fall under the jurisdiction of the King of Hell, free from the Wheel of Reincarnation), he orders his monkey friends to, 'tear down some old pines and make me a raft. Find a bamboo pole to punt with and load it up with fruit. I'm going'.

What troubled me throughout the *nong chao er* research was the lack of reference to the boards being ridden. Perhaps they used their poles with flags to balance and punt through sections? Perhaps they favoured the quality of a short ride, or rode different sections in different ways on different equipment - prone, bodysurfing or standing on boards, or using a pole. Of course, we know that the geography of the river has changed drastically since the Tang and Song, but witnessing the tidal bore I concluded that it was very unlikely the *nong chao er* were only swimming and bodysurfing. Perhaps some were, but that would have been a very hard technique to carry a flag that never got wet. I think they would have been commonly using boards to tread waves, riding prone or standing, and speaking with Mr Wu seemed to confirm this.

We gathered for a final dinner, went to bed exhausted, then woke early the next morning. We needed to be out by 8.00 am. As we cued up waiting to checkout from the hotel, the unfriendly receptionist greeted us with a rare smile. "I've got something for you guys," he said. He passed over a handful of newspapers. It was the

Hangzhou Youth Times. Emblazoned across the front page was a picture of our crew, and an article by Wang Xinke with the headline, 'Foreigners break the law, and a surfing world record'. Even if I didn't 'tread waves' myself, the trip suddenly felt like a success. I couldn't wait to share the news with Mr Wu. I found him aside the dam, fixing the engine of his boat. I held out the *Hangzhou Youth Times*. He jumped onto the concrete bank and hugged me with his greasy hands. "I saw you from the roof of the dam. I was so happy... and worried. They always tried to stop it, but the tide is stronger, stronger than any dam. You, and crazy Feng, are the tide." I immediately understood the reference to crazy Feng as the fisherman (or Buddhist monk) we saw running along the banks. "Crazy Feng. What was he doing?" "Crazy Feng was the best at wave treading. He would perform a hundred manoeuvres on his thin piece of wood. Police banned him from any activity inside the river. He now lives in a shack behind the dam and simply runs with it, living on whatever the tide gives him - carp, eels, birds. Some say he's just an unemployed lunatic. Others say he's the last *nong chao er*."

Hangzhou Youth Times, 27/10/2007

CHAPTER SEVENTEEN

WAVE BATH

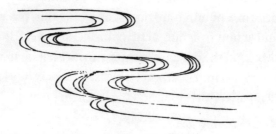

I arrived back in Italy, passport thankfully intact (meaning I'd be allowed to travel back to China undeterred), and chased a searing hot Sirocco swell to the Puglia coast with my new girlfriend Olga. It was bliss to get into the crystal blue, salty water of southern Italy after all the brown brackish mud of the Qiantang.

Back in Ravenna I proudly showed Guancia and the *SurfNews* crew the *Hangzhou Youth Times*. Guancia loved hearing about our travels to China, and I had a nice new bit of Maoist paraphernalia for him - a red Mao portrait pendant portraying the paramount leader in a bathing suit, right after a swim in the Yangtze. Mao is somehow considered the patron of taxi drivers and these are ubiquitous in China. Guancia placed it into his red VW Beetle with pride, certain that had Mao got the chance, he would have become a surfer.

I figured that it must have been irresistible for the *Hangzhou Youth Times* to run the photo of 'foreigners shooting the tide on the Qiantang Jiang'. This natural phenomena has been an irrepressible symbol for China. The anti-Qing (remember the Qing were the last dynasty) newspaper *Tide of Zhejiang* (*Zhejiang Chao*) founded in 1903 used the image of the Qiantang to symbolise the unstoppable tide of revolution that was sweeping over China in the late 19th century. And the leader of the movement that then led to the establishment of the Republic of China in 1912 (replacing the last dynasty), Sun Yat-sen, proclaimed, 'World progress is like a tidal wave. Those who ride it will prosper, and those who fight against it will perish'.

But soon in the 20th century as the promises of the Republican era were unfulfilled, 潮 *chao* was used to describe the 'angry tides' (怒潮 *nù cháo*) of worker protest, and expressions such as 'student surges' (學潮 *xúe cháo*) and 'worker surges' (工潮 *gōng cháo*) characterised the mass unrest. Then, as radical rural reform was encouraged and then imposed on the country in the early years of the People's Republic, Mao celebrated the 'high tide of socialism' (社會主義高潮 *shèhuìzhuyì gāo cháo*) that would transform rural China. Following Mao's death in 1976, the now more liberal Communist Party turned its attention to economic development and the move was spoken of in terms of a 'new historical tide': a place where modern surfing (冲浪 *chōn làng*) could enter the stage.

Throughout the *Hangzhou Youth Times* article we were not described as *nong chao er*, but 冲浪高手 *chōn làng gāoshou*, surfing experts, the modern Chinese word for 'surfing', quite simply meaning 'bathing + wave', 'wave bath', or more poetically 'entering the waves'. 冲 *Chōng*, for 'bathing', 'rinsing' or 'washing', implies an almost passive relationship with the wave, as 'entering the waves' or 'wave bath' suggested by the radical water 氵 aside the middle character 中 *zhōng* . But another interpretation from the military lexicon is immediate to all Chinese. *Chong* is also translatable with 'charging', 'rushing' and 'dashing', often used in 冲锋 *chōng fēng* which literally means 'dashing + tip of a blade', or 'engaging in battle'. 'Dashing waves' or 'charging waves' is another interpretation of the more extreme side of *chong lang*.

Nong chao er was however used elsewhere in the paper in another article about business. In China today a *nong chao er* (interpreted in this context as a 'tide player') is used to describe an entrepreneur who has taken advantage of the 'great tidal surge of commerce' (商業大潮 *shāngyè dà cháo*) to make their fortune, explored closely in US-based writer Jianying Zha's book titled*Tide Players: The Movers and Shakers of a Rising China*. Similarly, the phrase 下海 *xià hai* ('go into the sea') is used to describe those who work in the private and foreign sectors and get rich in the 'tides of commerce'. But *xia hai* is also defined as 'to go into prostitution' and 退潮 *tuì cháo* ('receding tide') is used in equal measure with 'go into the sea' as a reminder of the disappointment that invariably follows in the wake of economic and political opportunism. The *yin* and *yang* is ever-present in China. Yet into the more open and opportunistic economy of post Mao China (and the potential for an emerging middle class of youth with time and money on their side) extreme sports would inevitably start to have a wider audience (also the foundation for surfing booms in California in the 1950s, Japan in the 1970s and South Korea in the 2010s). As a fan of extreme swimming, Mao might have been keen to try surfing himself. Nevertheless, during the open door policy of the late 1970s, sports gained youth interest, and sometimes state funding if they could lead to prestigious Olympic gold and national pride.

Faced with translations of classic 'western sports' (many of which were already introduced in the early 1900s) China took a pragmatic and literal approach: basketball became 篮球 *lán qíu* (basket + ball) and football became 足球 *zú qíu* (foot + ball). An entry for 'surfing' as *'chong lang'* (wave + bath) had in fact also been in some Chinese dictionaries since the early 1900s, but the first traces in the Chinese media appeared in late 1970s on youth oriented programs broadcast on the national TV station showcasing 'novelties from the West'. The flavour of these kinds of shows that celebrated western ideas was interesting. The most daring and controversial was *River Elegy* in 1988 (the year I started at University) that debated live onscreen how China could learn from the West about modernisation and democracy. The show used the analogy of the Yellow River, now dried up, needing renewal from the 'flowing blue seas of the west'. The directors criticised the legacy of Mao's Cultural Revolution and celebrated American popular culture. Yellow symbolised stagnation, blue, an ocean of Western thinking. But after the social turmoils of 1989 the more radical media approaches were censored, the show was axed and it's producers forced into exile. As a student in Venice at the time, we also noticed a re-tightening of the Communist grip through educational mantras.

Windsurfing - 帆板 *fānbǎn* (sail + board) - was also included in these youth shows, which had an immediate impact, perhaps because of it's a growing status as an Olympic sport. The story of windsurfing in China would make a book in itself, but a little information is worth sharing for the context of surfing. The government set up the Qingdao Sailing Sport School in Shandong province in 1979 (overseen by the governing Sports and Physical Culture Commission) and one of the coaches called Wang Li even started producing wood and resin boards using bamboo masts and fabric sails. There were soon national windsurfing competitions in Qingdao, other government funded schools in Zhejiang, Guangxi, Guangdong and Fujian provinces, and China entered a windsurf team for the windglider discipline at the 1984 Olympics in Los Angeles. Later that year Zhang Xiaodong from Guangdong province won the women's triangle race at the World Windsurfing Championships in Perth, Australia, and went on to win a silver medal in one of the windsurfing disciplines at the 1992 Olympics in Barcelona. This was considered a huge success story for Chinese windsurfing, justifying government funding, and a number of international champions have since followed.

Had the cultural history of the *nong chao er* not been suppressed from the popular imagination due to the dangers and banning of the activity on the Qiantang, perhaps the producers of these TV shows might have made sweeping claims linking Chinese wave-riding to Polynesian surfing. After all, it wouldn't take much to stretch the imagination of a nationalist that while pre-Han Chinese from the Wu-Yue area were among the first to adopt agriculture and set out into the Pacific, surfing might have travelled with them. Of course this is a far-fetched claim. The Wu-Yue people set out in the migration between 2000 and 1000 BC. While the oldest mention we have of the Qiantang tidal wave is in the *History of the Southern States of Wu and Yue*, compiled during the Han Dynasty and the first evidence of the *nong chao er* active in Hangzou is from the 9th century, by which point surfing had evolved into a complex cultural practice in Polynesia. We know also that wave-riding has evolved independently in South America, Africa and South Asia. But perhaps more will be revealed about the ancient practice of the *nong chao er* as more people research the unrivalled depth of China's historical documents.

Despite the impact of *fan ban* (windsurfing), by the early 2000s the vast majority of Chinese were completely unfamiliar with the word *chong lang*. Even the phrase 'surfing the net' is different in China. 'Fishing' is the reference instead of 'surfing'. 'Going online' is 上网 *shàng wǎng* which literally means 'going on the net', where the knots inside the character 网 imply communication between people. The word *chong lang* certainly gained wider attention in 2007 when the American animation movie *Surf's Up* got widely distributed and subtitled. Then big changes for all sports happened the following year when Beijing hosted the 2008 Olympics. This stimulated even wider acceptance and funding platforms for emerging sports, and a new funding model combining centralised government and private clubs and sports marketing agencies and brands emerged. Within the Sports and Physical Culture Commission, the Chinese Extreme Sports Association (CESA) had been established in 2004, but by 2008 it had the budget, private company collaborations and political muscle to begin to facilitate the 'first' (if you exclude the Mid-Autumn Festivals of the Song) state sponsored surf events in China.

As global river bore riding continued to grow in popularity, it was inevitable that more foreign surfers would be attracted to the mighty Silver Dragon. It appeared that our efforts in 2007 didn't go unnoticed, and in 2008 CESA (directed by Wei Xing) and the sports marketing and manufacturing brand Wabsono (lead by Glenn Brumage and Bao Xuping), invited some international professional surfers on a reconnaissance trip to scout the Qiantang Jiang. Americans Mike Cianciulli and Brad Gerlach surfed the bore in the city limits of Hangzhou, raised great media coverage, and assured the Chinese government that the Silver Dragon was rideable (by 'modern surfing standards'). The following month Mike Cianciulli returned with Greg and Rusty Long and Mark Healey to put on an exhibition at the Mid-Autumn Festival when over 300,000 people lined the banks of the Qiantang Jiang. Rusty Long even got barrelled on one section (surely to the joy of Mr Wu and Crazy Feng), and the event was broadcast to over 500 million through the leading national TV news station *CCTV*.

In that same year the first official organisation, *Surfing China*, was created in Hangzhou to promote surfing and its industry in mainland China under the recognition of the Water Sports Administration Centre, and of the International Surfing Association (ISA). The first summit (Surfing China Expo) was held in Hangzhou in May 2009. More than one hundred experts from China and abroad gathered to discuss the possibilities of developing the surf industry in China.

The obvious media success encouraged the government to support an annual event, where, for a few days a year, the illegal activity of riding the river bore could be lifted for the invitees who performed in small teams. The first event only had permission to ride the urban sections of the river, a total of 10 km in Hangzhou municipality. But quickly authorities allowed the newly branded 'Qiantang Shootout' to extend eastwards all the way to Bridge Number Nine, just past the Bore Watching Resort, where the wave starts to break best. But it turns out that the Qiantang wasn't the first time the government invited foreign surfers into China for reconnaissance. Enter Hainan Island, the tail of the dragon.

Photo courtesy: Battle at Silver Dragon/Wabsono

CHAPTER EIGHTEEN

SUN MOON BAY

Hainan - an oval shaped sub-tropical island in the South China Sea, just south of Guangdong province - was known as the enigmatic outer limit of the Han Empire and the southernmost limit of Chinese authority, caricatured as the end of the Earth or the tail of the dragon throughout Chinese history. The island was perceived by most ruling dynasties as an unpopulated area suitable for exiles, despite the fact the ethnic Li people, descendants of the ancient Wu-Yue tribes from the mainland, had settled here 3,000 years ago. Perhaps the secluded nature of Hainan made it optimal for a surfing experiment. And a few years before Stuart Matthews' ground-breaking Qiantang expedition in 1988, the eccentric and flamboyant Australian professional surfer Peter Drouyn trained a small team of Chinese athletes in Hainan on the first government funded project.

According to research by Jamie Brisick in the book *Becoming Westerly: surf champion Peter Drouyn's transformation into Westerly Windina,* Drouyn had read Asian Studies at Brisbane's Griffith University, studied sinology and picked up some Mandarin. Dejected by prospects in the surfing powerhouses of Australia and America (where he'd been a competitive pioneer for two decades), Drouyn became inspired by the idea of training a Chinese surf team to competition glory. In fact, he was convinced that surfing would be an Olympic sport, and that the Chinese could become world champions. So he wrote to the Sports and Physical Culture Commission at the Chinese government proposing that he train a team. They responded positively, most likely due to the parallels with windsurfing (which was enjoying competitive success and national pride), and invited Drouyn to Hainan in 1985.

Drouyn prepared boards, surf lessons in Mandarin, and was presented with 25 students. One of them, Wang Yongjian, would later become a close friend of mine and a key player in the contemporary development of surfing in China. Meanwhile, the local authorities carefully scouted Hainan island on a 60 day long trip and concluded that the municipality of Wanning, on the central east coast, had the most suitable waves for the project.

Wang, and 14 of the other students, were aged 18-20 and from windsurf backgrounds (already in the national team) selected from Shandong, Zhejiang, Guangxi, Guangdong and Fujian. Ten local younger kids were from Hainan attending a government Sports School. Wang explained that "the expectation was for the windsurfers to become surf coaches, who could then set up surf schools around the nation, and start developing the sport like we did with windsurfing."

"We all met in Haikou," explained Wang, "and spent four days taking theory class and watching surfing movies. Our coach (Peter Drouyn) told us that the plan was to train a team and beat the Australians and Americans. Then we travelled by bus to a government run guest-house in Wanning. Every day we drove to the beach at Riyue Wan."

With the narrative of the tidal bores so prevalent in the ancient history of wave-riding in China, it was fitting that this experiment for modern surfing happened at a place named after the very driver of tides - the sun and the moon. 日月湾, Rì yuè wān, Sun Moon Bay, is a butter yellow beach with a long and luscious left pointbreak on the east coast of the island, halfway between Haikou and Sanya.

Wang Yongjian continued, "There was no hotel, or road in, so we parked behind the large sand dunes and walked to the beach. Mr Drouyn could not speak Chinese, so an interpreter was organised for the lessons on the beach. But having got to know surfing more closely as I got older, I know that so many of the important points were lost in translation. After one week, none of us could stand up. The main problem was that all Mr Drouyn's longer boards had been denied embarking on the flight and never made it into the country, so we only had around ten shortboards, all about 7'0" long. The waves were very small, so shortboards were near impossible to learn on. Mr Drouyn did not push us on whitewater, like instructors do today, and instead taught us how to paddle out and then try to catch waves with him. Some stood for a few seconds. Most never even got close. The waves did not break at the point like they do on larger swells at Riyue Wan. We all realised the learning curve was longer than expected, and so did our leaders. That's one of the very special qualities of surfing - it's so hard to learn. But the authorities started to conclude that the project was irrelevant. Yet we were intrigued by how Mr Drouyn spoke about getting in rhythm with the ocean, something we knew from windsurfing and Daosim. He taught us how to bodysurf, and I've since enjoyed the skills I picked up from him for my whole life."

"The program lasted two weeks and we only surfed at Riyue Wan" said Wang. "Then we got sent home as our involvement in the project was ended. From the windsurf team that went, no-one continued surfing until equipment and other surfers started to appear 20 years later. When I returned to my windsurf team in Yantai, Shandong province, I did try to ride waves in the northeast swell, but our windsurfers were too long and designed for speed sailing, so without the right equipment, it was impossible to control them in the waves. If I had the right equipment, I might have got into it."

"I don't know exactly why the project stopped," Wang concluded. "But I think there were differences in the vision of the authorities and Mr Drouyn. The authorities wanted him to train local coaches that could grow into a project on a national scale. Mr Drouyn wanted a group of talented young kids under his training schedule to beat the best in West. But above all I think communication was a problem, and the slow learning curve of surfing."

The 1985 surf experiment fits into the wider context of tourism development in Hainan. Domestic beach resorts had been prevalent in China since the 1920s, but between 1949 and 1974 under Maoism, China was closed to all but a handful of foreigners. Deng Xiaoping's open door policy of the late 1970s changed that radically as tourism was seen as an opportunity to earn foreign exchange. In 1985 1.4 million foreigners visited China generating $1.3 billion in revenue. Peter Drouyn's proposal likely looked an exciting opportunity for the authorities, combining both tourism and sport. Sub-tropical Hainan was the perfect location: 1,580 km of clear-water coastline, where long stretches of sand are divided by headlands, hot springs, and a backdrop of volcanic mountains. Add the consistent small waves, botanical gardens and mountainside coffee-houses, and you had a perfect location to attract massive tourism investment. Above all, this is the only part of China that is warm all year.

The 1980s tourism development plan was to market Hainan as the 'Chinese Hawaii'. In a savvy marketing scheme, Hainan and Hawaii became 'sister states' and Maui and Sanya 'sister counties'. In the early 1990s a number of tourism business pioneers were invited from Maui to Sanya to exchange ideas. One of these was American architect and surfer David Greenberg, a world-renowned specialist in designing treehouses, usually with bamboo. Hainan's government was so excited by David's treehouses that they commissioned him to design one in Sanya's Nanshan area at the birth of the region's tourist boom. Hainan was soon being advertised throughout China (and Russia) as a 'tropical paradise', attracting millions of tourists every year, mainly to Sanya. As Hainan tourism was developing, high rise hotels were also juxta-posed to a number of future-facing projects led by David Green-berg and his philosophy of local community led development. 'Hawaiian surfing' would fit in naturally, as it has done in many other tourism areas around the planet, from Bali to Barbados.

Of course other international surfers explored Hainan in the 1980s and 1990s. A notable trip was in 1986 with Hawaiian-Chi-nese surf legend Rell Sunn, and Americans Matt George and pho-tographer Warren Bolster, spearheaded by *Surfer* magazine editor Paul Holmes and months of diplomacy from the president of an international non-profit consulting company who had strong links with American Chinese consulates and organisations pro-moting beach tourism in Hainan. But travel was heavily restricted and this was not Indonesia, therefore the marketing in magazine features was never going to attract large numbers of tube-hun-gry surf travellers overnight. Yet Chinese surfing started to grow slowly in the 1990s, first out of Hong Kong, which hosted surf contests by 1997 (whereas Taiwan had their first American-influ-enced locals as early as the 1960s).

By the millennium, masses of surf equipment was already being manufactured in China, and Hainan was destined to de-velop a local scene. Japanese surfer Hiroshi Yonekawa was a pi-oneer, setting up the Monran surf factory in Haikou (producing surfboards for the Japanese market) in the mid 1990s. He started to host adventurous longboarders who were keen to escape the frigid northwest Pacific winters and the overcrowded spots close to Tokyo. Riyue Wan was the go to spot, and Hiroshi Yonekawa christened the long left point 'Yarakawa', Japanese for 'slow wave' and perfect for the rising popularity of longboarding. By the early

2000s the Japanese visitors had inspired a small number of local surfers in Haikou, Sanya and Riyue Wan.

By now, the minister of tourism for Hainan, Zhou Ping, had travelled to Maui a number of times and developed a good friendship with David Greenberg. David suggested to Zhou the idea of Hainan having festivals celebrating surfing, art and the culture of the island's ethnic Li people. Zhou and David conceived a plan for small-scale 'bottom up' surf tourism development celebrating what already exists and was successful and iconic, such as the grass-roots surf clubs that had already developed. It took a while for these plans to come to fruition, but the seeds were sown and the Beijing Olympics in 2008 would provide the economic impetus to invest in alternative sports.

Callahan explored Hainan in 2001 with Sam Bleakley and South African Duncan Scott, and in 2004 Antony Colas researched the island for the *World Stormrider Guide* writing a comprehensive entry. I had even run a couple of articles in *SurfNews* magazine on Hainan before I first visited in 2006 during the trip where I travelled on to Yunnan and the Qiongzhu Temple. I criss-crossed Hainan by local buses, usually filled with ethnic Li carrying produce between markets and villages. My board was often resting on top of sacks of cabbage and rice. Surfers were completely alien to the island, and the tourism construction boom was in its infancy. But even though there was only a dirt road into Riyue Wan, there was now a surreal mix of tourism provisions developed in the late 1980s and early 1990s: a chain hotel, some villas, camel and horse rides, newly built statues, restaurants and a visitor complex with a large sign in English proclaiming: 'Tourist people is god, and this place is heaven. If you are satisfied, then heaven will be beautiful'.

Riyue Wan had changed dramatically since Drouyn surfed there. Wang Yongjian remembered "no buildings, no palm trees and massive sand dunes we had to park behind to walk to the beach." Development of a new highway linking Haikou and Sanya had flattened the sand dunes. By 2006 bus loads of Chinese tourists would arrive every weekend in Riyue Wan on a guided tour through the island. But there was just a handful of local surfers, focused on the undeveloped opposite end of the bay and a long left pointbreak over-looked by a haunting unfinished and abandoned hotel, aptly named 'Ghost Hotel'. I only scored small swell when I visited, so I surfed the beachbreak, and met a few of the local surfers who'd learned from visiting Japanese. Without scoring the quality rides on the point on a good swell it was easy for Riyue Wan to not register on the surf travel radar.

I flew out of Sanya to Hong Kong, before travelling inland, sure I'd be back to Hainan in the future. By 2007 there was a solid scene in Sanya, including Zhang Dahai, Darci Liu and Monica Guo, and some expats from Australia and California. Then American Brendan Sheridan started the annual Surfing Hainan Open contest at Riyue Wan in 2008. Californian longboarding legend Robert 'Wingnut' Weaver - co-star of Bruce Brown's 1994 classic *The Endless Summer II* - attended the event, and started to visit regularly, inspiring all the locals. The heart of the Riyue Wan grassroots scene by then was 'Mama's' fish restaurant, run by Huang Wen, Huang Ning, Huang Li and their rotund 'Mama' (Wang Aizhu). She was famed for wearing outlandish leopard skin print t-shirts and tie-died pants, cowboy hat and Wellington boots. The family made great food - garlic-fried shrimps, coconut rice, squid, red snapper and spinach leaves, noodle soup, boiled Wenchang chicken, spicy chilli tofu, and congee soup, all washed down by *Tsingtao* beer. And the youngest son Huang Wen developed an electric enthusiasm for longboarding, teeth stained from chewing *binglang* (betel nut), which the family farmed in the forest behind the beach.

The emerging scene quickly figured out that November to March was the prime season for the long left point. Most travellers thus far had been looking to score Hainan on a fickle late summer typhoon swell, unaware of the reliability and quality of waves during the northeast monsoon. On it's day Riyue Wan could be a snaking, overhead, surprisingly good 200 metres long ride, blowing offshore by the same wave producing northeast wind. In the summer between May and September they could surf the south facing beachbreaks all the way to Sanya. And the typhoon season from August to October could deliver spectacular waves anywhere on the island, or a devastating direct hit. They also started to explore a feast of other left pointbreaks north and south where the northeast wind blew offshore.

In opportunistic style, the regional Wanning government formulated a plan to help popularise local surfing by having an annual surf festival at Riyue Wan. But first Zhou Ping wanted to invite a reconnaissance team to scout the potential surf breaks in Wanning. It was typical Chinese style to consult experts in the field when dealing with something new, with the aim to then integrate the learning into a wider plan. A new generation of politicians and business backers apparently had no idea about the first two-month-long scouting of 1985, Peter Drouyn's project, or the Rell Sunn and the *Surfer* magazine trip, a couple of generations back. But China was now a much different economy, with a huge and youthful middle class hungry for beach holidays and action sports. A Shanghai based sports agency called *Uist Sports* was hired, and Callahan was contacted to photograph a surf crew of Californians Holly Beck, Kim Mayor and Wingnut along with Emi Cataldi, Erwan Simon and Sam Bleakley. They were officially invited as the 'International Site Inspection Team' to explore and document the Wanning coast, publish articles, and then partake in the inaugural Wanning International Surfing Festival, that was going to be combined with the Hainan Open, then grow into an independent event (soon hosting annual Association of Surfing Professionals / World Surf League world longboard titles and International Surfing Association shortboard events).

I was invited on the return trip by *Uist Sports* and the Wanning government to work as a translator and announcer at the montage of press conferences, surf demonstrations, seminars and dinners, culminating in the surf festival. Having entertained Chinese business elites in Italy for a long time, I was more than familiar with the endless speeches and ritual toasts to celebrate cultural exchange. *Gan bei* ('dry glass' or 'bottoms up') is demanded after every course. A Chinese proverb says, 'if you leave a social meal sober you did not truly enjoy yourself'. Needless to say, we all enjoyed ourselves at a time when the global surf industry was starting to stagnate and advertising revenue at *SurfNews* (and magazines throughout Europe, America and Australia) was beginning to dry up.

There was a lavish opening ceremony to the inaugural Wanning International Surfing Festival just north of Riyue Wan at Shimei Wan (close to another great left pointbreak), broadcast live on *CCTV*. That night at the hotel party at the swanky *Le Meridien* Wingnut introduced me to the team developing the river bore event - Glenn Brumage and Bao Xuping from *Wabsono* and CESA director Wei Xing. I knew all about the art of *guan xi* - personal, government and business networks usually lubricated by alcohol - and ordered an expensive round of mojitos as we all sat in the jacuzzi to talk. I told them all the story from the 2007 trip and apologised to Wei Xing for having broken the law. We quickly formed a good friendship and they invited me to judge at the newly branded 'Qiantang Shootout' the following year.

That night I realised the strange serendipity: my Chinese name *Li Jianhao* given to me by Professor Yang at University in

Venice decades earlier turned out to be a linguistic prophecy. Where the character 健 *Jiàn* ('valiant', 'healthy', 'strong' but also 'inflexible') portrays a line of soldiers being inspected by an official (the radical 亻 on the left), 豪 *háo* means 'hero', the same word used by Zhou Mi while referring to the *nong chao er* and the river wave being 'worthy of brave heroes'. So one translation of my Chinese nickname could be 'the inflexible judge inspecting the heroes'. And that suddenly applied to what I would start to do at the Qiantang Shootout. I'd somehow got the role of assigning the silver prizes to the 'brave watermen from Wu'. But I'd not yet been truly lured by the coastline of China. Riyue Wan was a good wave, yet I was battling it with crowds of travelling professionals and looking for some surfing solitude to pull me into an untapped side of Hainan.

CHAPTER EIGHTEEN — SUN MOON BAY

CHAPTER NINETEEN

GHOST HOTEL

Frustrated with the competitive crowds freesurfing the main point at Riyue Wan at the inaugural Wanning International Surfing Festival in 2010, Emi Cataldi suggested we have a secret session at the beach break behind the so-called Ghost Hotel, an abandoned building half-built in the late 1980s that overlooks the bay. On the last trip a month earlier Emi and crew had scored smoking five star waves here, and a few barrels.

Shortboard underarm, and a few croissants stashed inside my backpack from the five star *Le Meridien* hotel breakfast buffet, I panted uphill, then stopped to turn around and contemplate a stunning set of waves caressing the point. "It's always twice this size on the other side Zanella," said Emi, addressing me by my surname to stress the need to get moving. "Tide is filling in. Let's go."

The walkway soon aimed at an unguarded gate, before disappearing under our feet into the remains of a vast overgrown park, part of the original hotel property that was privately funded without government permits, ran out of money and abandoned. We tracked in knee-deep grass, through the paved terrace, composed of heavy limestone tiles, some broken by the roots of towering coconut trees. Impenetrable mangroves had capsized ornamental statues, unrecognisable clay features of dynastic dignitaries, toppled from the sea-facing fence. They lay beheaded on the lower terrace, their winged Confucian hats flipped over and engulfed in young tropical fern.

On the last steep ascent to the Ghost Hotel we flanked dozens of cylindrical rice grinders carved in red granite. They offered the perfect habitat for huge tarantulas and their beastly webs. This was a typically ambitious Chinese build - taking heavy decorations, each over 1,000 kilograms in weight, one kilometre up the hill, and never even finishing the main building. Shocked by the apparent futility of it all, we covered the last bit of the now thick jungle track, waving our boards through the bush to scare the tarantulas.

Then finally out of the foliage and on top of the cliff, we ventured into the abandoned Ghost Hotel, scaling up the spiralling stairway to the rooftop view. This would make a perfect setting for a film noir, the structure exposing its iron soul, like the emaciated rib cage of a sick giant, bent by its own static mass, condemned to rot away in the forest. If you stop at the surface, if you give up right away, places like Ghost Hotel represent China at its worst, showing the dirty shades behind glittering megastructures. But after enough trips to this country, after committing to its language and culture, I know that the pace of change here is so frantic that you cannot afford to feel passionate for buildings or objects. You learn to enjoy things in the present, you witness them as they flourish, or burn away, and let them go, just like waves: no tears and no claims. This is the price to pay for a better, more positive interaction with China. And this attitude can lead you to unexpected amazing places, lifelong friendships, and in this case, also perfect surf. The Ghost Hotel is just a project that was never finished, but now offers an unrivalled view of the Wanning coastline.

We popped up from the last vertical ladder in blinding midday light, 25 metres up and way above the flora below. Blue ocean corduroy stretched out to the horizon. "*Da paura*," said Emi, a typical Roman allocution meaning both awesome and frightening at once. We soaked in the view, our pupils finally adjusting to the glare. Looking south, China's most advanced surf tourism experiment,

The Wanning International Surfing Festival, was in full swing, the main point bustling with pro surfers from all over the world. The government had made a massive push to prepare Riyue Wan - new roads, new buildings, new veneers, and new surf clubs and surf shops planned. The speed and scale was mind-boggling. This was a 'can do' mentality in action. Endorsed by Beijing's central government, the head of CESA, Mr Wei Xing, and Zhou Ping from the Ministry of Hainan Tourism, were at the forefront of deals being signed with the International Surfing Association (ISA) and Association of Surfing Professionals ASP (soon to become the World Surf League (WSL)). Local investment funds, real estate developers, environment conscious architects and surfers were all jostling for a piece of the pie.

But looking north, away from the hustle-and-bustle, kilometres of deserted surf heaven unfolded. The coastline here was pristine. This was the China that was luring me in. "Bingo," erupted Emi as a wave hit a sand bank and left a perfect triangle of whitewater in its wake. "Must be at least head high on the sets. And look at that spit," he added as the third wave in the set unloaded.

The smell on top of the canopy hit my nostrils like a jab: marshes, pine trees and flowers, with a salty aftertaste. "Emi, this place smells just like Ravenna under a northeast swell." The northeast monsoon hits Hainan after slicing the entire continent northeast to southwest for over 5,000 km. While it generates swell through wind fetch across a long stretch of East and South China Sea, it also blows in a wide enough belt to pick up a variety of unique smells from China's vast landmass. It matures its aromas as it runs away from the sub polar steppe of the Amur Basin and Inner Mongolia, and breaks into the lowlands surrounding the Yangtze River. From here it heads straight down to Henan, Hubei, Hunan and Guangdong: through a megalopolis surrounded by rice fields, rivers, marshes and fish farms. There is no mountain chain to block the wind's course, nor alter its organoleptic affair with China's soggy, rich, rice-yielding womb.

The last notable scents are acquired locally on the high gorges of Mount Wuzhi, Hainan's tallest peak at 1,840 metres. Then, just before striking the surf the monsoon is enriched with the minty notes of endemic *pinus fenzeliana*, a majestic, resinous white pine that has adapted to subtropical weather but was born in the mountains of Guangxi and Guizhou, 1,000 km north on the mainland. The final touch in this cocktail was the fruity bouquet given by mango groves, papayas, bananas and betel nut palms, grown in orchards just behind the beach.

Small, compact anthracite coloured stratocumuli rushed down the mountains, and quickly blew out at sea. A thick maritime bush drew a brown line between the apricot hues of the dunes and the dark green wall of semi-cultivated jungle. The ocean was azure and white with the foam trails of breaking waves. Ochre granite outcrops dotted the shoreline, as if dropped there from outer space: ferrous barnacles dressed in fancy foam.

Stretching north, not a soul was in sight. "It looks like Hawaii, but smells like home," I said to Emi. Inhale, exhale, my body quickly synched with the *fengshui* of the place, my lower abdomen starting to squirm, producing that tactile feeling of fear and excitement that commonly precedes an epic surf session or a deep *Taiji* practice.

As bigger and better waves started breaking we headed down from the roof to the ground floor. We used tree branches for a faster slide to the beach, selected the hollowest peak, and jumped into liquid bliss. The South China Sea is to the Pacific Ocean what the Mediterranean is to the Atlantic. They both have traits in common with their massive neighbour. Pacific-style long lulls

241

between good waves followed by oversized sets (every 20 minutes or so) are the norm in Hainan. The difference with Mediterranean swells, so Atlantic in their impetuosity and fast pace, was striking. The ocean here goes *yin* flat after every big *yang* set of waves, allowing you to easily paddle back out to the take-off zone. This scenario is tailor-made for two friends sharing waves alone: tell a story, catch a wave, repeat. *Yang* and *yin*.

The waves proved to be as powerful as they looked from above: short racy pockets of energy, hitting the sand just 50 meters from the beach, allowing for three fast manoeuvres before extinguishing all their fury in a thundering shore pound. We started tapping on that *yang* like never before, then chatting between sets during the long *yin* lulls. Emi had just broken up with his Italian girlfriend and moved full-time to live and work in Australia as a hot-air balloon engineer in Byron Bay. I had just married Olga in Italy. We had both opened new chapters in our lives and had not surfed together since our last expedition to North Africa, two years ago.

Emi's surfing had improved heaps since our last session together. With world class waves on his doorstep in Australia and half a dozen West Africa projects under his belt with Callahan, his style had flourished in a way that would have been unattainable at his home spot Ostia (aka 'the village'), Rome's surf hub and fancy summer resort. "You didn't surf like that back in the village," I said after witnessing another one of his vertical moves and fans of spray. We continued to trade sets, share stories and laugh out aloud.

Half an hour into the session a set came in with not a drop of water out of place. Emi was on the inside paddling back out. It was my wave. I took off easily, sliding into trim. Then the wave started sucking brown sand up the face as it zipped down the sand bar, doubled in size and produced a thick, plunging lip. The wall morphed into a wide, almond shaped pit that engulfed me whole. I caressed the face with my back arm, aimed my nose to the open door and enjoyed the incredible view. Sun rays filtered through the cascading lip, casting a jade-green light inside. I could see layers of colour through the falling curtain: azure, yellow, green, blurring into each other like oil paint. Then a void. I hung in there, in non-action, for as long as I could, then got spat out, my body hair straightened by the endorphin rush. This was the wave I needed to inspire me to finally move to China.

"I think this place likes you man," yelled Emi, who had seen the ride from the channel and was now hooting like a madman. "I want to move here. They are talking about a national surf club, to be opened here in Riyue Bay, and a lot of events to work at as a translator, plus a national surf team to help train. Plus there is an annual river bore event in Hangzhou - The Qiantang Shootout. I think there will be plenty of work for me." Emi knew about my research into the *nong chao er*. He knew that my relationship with China was love-like and that this was my big opportunity. "Welcome to Asia," he replied. We clumsily hugged each other while sitting on our boards. It was a vow. "And what about Olga?" said Emi, scratching his head and changing tone. "Mellow left-handers, she'll love it here, and it will be a nice chance to start something new together." "It's going to be very hard for her," said Emi. "It's the biggest culture shock you can think of." Emi was right.

Olga was born and raised between central Milan, Sicily's southern coast, and the hills of Maremma in Tuscany. Following our wedding she had quit her job as a staff journalist at *Donna Di Repubblica*, Italy's most stylish fashion weekly, and moved to Ravenna to live together and focus on teaching yoga and surfing. She loved beauty in all its forms, be it buildings, design or literature, and she was interested in China, learning some basic Mandarin at the Confucius Institute in Milan. But of course she didn't feel the same passion I felt for this culture. She had only shared the Italian side of me in our four years together, and she had appeared scared of my Chinese side, right from the get go, especially my obsession with the *nong chao er*.

I knew that moving to China was going to be a jump into a void, a game changer for our relationship. But I had spent most of my life preparing for this chance, attending University in Venice in the turbulent 1980s, working as a Mandarin interpreter in the glitzy 1990s, running *SurfNews* magazine during the European surf boom of the 2000s (that now felt like it was waning), learning about the *nong chao er,* and now exploring a new frontier of Asian surfing, with the best in the field.

I envisioned this opportunity as a big approaching wave, capping up right there at the beachbreak we called Ghost Hotel, and breaking down the line. At this stage I was still figuring out my positioning, trying to understand what line to hold, what sections to avoid, and who to align with. I had dreams and doubts. But I was sure of one thing: I was going to paddle with all my strength, catch this wave, and ride it, no matter how big or how steep it turned out to be.

In the year ahead I flew to Hainan six times, working freelance as a translator, announcer and contest staff for the ISA and ASP/WSL. Between jobs I surfed my brains out in far better waves than I ever dreamed I'd find in China. The secret was recognising the northeast monsoon as the prime season for countless empty left pointbreaks. Importantly, I secured opportunities for full time work. At one of the WSL events Wingnut took me down to a fishing village called 后海 Hòuhǎi ('Back Sea' - or 藤海 Ténghǎi to the old locals), located north of Sanya and south of Riyue Wan, and facing straight into that same smell/swell that had enchanted me on top of Ghost Hotel. Wingnut had been there in 2008 during his first trip to Hainan with the local surf crew from Sanya. I immediately liked this Chinese version of Taghazout in Morocco, with its narrow streets and atmospheric crumbling old buildings. With a population of about 2,000 it was much bigger and more vibrant than Riyue Wan, so I knew it was a better place for Olga and I. Consequently, in early 2011 I left my best board there in Houhai at *Nanuna*, the first surf hotel that had just opened, sure I'd be returning soon.

Back in Italy, Olga and I travelled to Venice on a bitterly cold winter weekend to talk about the idea of moving to Hainan together. She was onboard. We did some sightseeing, and in the Correr Museum Olga noticed Hainan on a *mappa mundi* from 1680 by geographer Vincenzo Coronelli. I recognised a few places I was getting to know near Riyue Wan, like Linsui (now Lingshui), Lingnan (now Lingwan). And then I spotted Tengqiao (near Houhai). Tengqiao means 'Rattan Cane Bridge', named when the place was only accessible by sea or through a rickety bridge across the river behind the village. I knew that the locals still called it this name and it was inscribed on a stone plaque at the village entrance. We both agreed this was the sign we needed to move to Houhai. *SurfNews* had successfully navigated the prime years of advertising support from the European surf industry, and we had mapped and surfed over 300 spots in Italy, opening the country to surf development, so we ended the magazine, proud of our achievements and the legacy we left for Italian surfers. With no strings attached in Italy, I left Ravenna with Olga in April 2011. China was our new life.

CHAPTER NINETEEN — GHOST HOTEL

CHAPTER TWENTY

THE PEOPLE'S REPUBLIC OF EMPTY WAVES

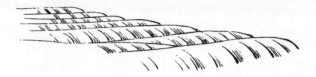

Houhai became our new home in no time. The lure of this village was that the road ended here. You arrived because you wanted to arrive, not by chance. You had to commit to this place. Every newcomer you met here was either escaping something or starting something new. Olga committed wholeheartedly to Houhai, but soon the language barrier proved too much and China killed our love. Olga was much happier in Italy. I was much happier in China. And we could not find a compromise. Olga moved back to Milan and we divorced. Thankfully we kept a strong friendship. But China had already won my heart. And I knew deep down that had I not turned my board and took off on that wave that day with Emi at Ghost Hotel, had I not taken the chance and moved to Hainan, questions of 'what if' would have haunted me forever. I took the drop, some might say to drown in the China Sea, but for me it was a chance to re-surface for a new life to begin.

The broad sweep of Houhai offered a good variety of waves, from a rocky, shallow left point working on solid northeast swells, to a stretch of beach break peaks, and a world class right-hander that breaks during typhoon swells. I could not find any written history of Houhai. It had a perfect natural deepwater harbour, and therefore was the first Chinese territory where ships could stop heading north from the Maluku 'Spice Islands' and Indonesia before the mainland ports. It was clearly important enough to warrant an appearance on Vincenzo Coronelli's *mappa mundi* in 1680.

However, the significance of Houhai must have waned because a story circulated around the village that it was only occupied seasonally as a fishing and trading base until fishing families from Danjia, in Guangdong province settled here permanently in the early 19th century. Then more and more families joined their relatives escaping the turmoil of the Opium Wars. Remote Houhai seemed far safer. But without their so-called ancestral tablets (or spirit tablets) that linked them to their forefathers in the ancestral village, the neighbouring Hainanese islanders (including the ethnic Li) were cautious of this village occupied by 'hostile outsiders with no homeland'.

Curiously, the first travelling outsiders that started to frequent the town were surfers. Then when the adjacent Wuzhizhou Island was developed as a tourist attraction, thousands of Chinese tourists started to arrive to take a ferry to the small butterfly-shaped island and enjoy its exotic gardens and marine ecology. Over 2,700 plant varieties are present on the island, and a travelling Daoist priest named Wu Huancan built a house here in the Qing dynasty claiming he'd found the elixir of life. A visitor complex was built on the outskirts of town, but only occasionally did tourists venture into Houhai's main streets to eat at restaurants. Also, during the Japanese Occupation, a network of secret submarine ports and military bases was constructed around Houhai, ultimately managed by the Chinese army, and now covered in thick verdant jungle, forming a natural barrier to the development of the area. There was however a rather imposing quarry nearby that let out tectonic explosions every now and then, frightening the living daylights out of the uninitiated. When I moved in, tourism, fishing and mining were the lifeblood of the economy.

Houhai east side, close to the harbour, is where the old locals lived. The west side, close to the beach, was the surfers side. Locals used to throw garbage and construction debris along the west side beach, but the surfers initiated a cleaning campaign to remove all the garbage and debris. As a result it was soon lined with low rise privately owned guesthouses, a reminder that Chinese beach fronts are not all filled with high rise hotels. The first, *Nanuna*, was set up by Qiu Han, an entrepreneur from Chengdu, taught to surf by Sanya based Hainan pioneer Zhang Dahai. Bitten by the surf bug, Qiu Han dreamed of finding a secluded tropical beach with his young son Qiu Zhuo to build a small Mediterranean style hotel for surfers and anyone looking to escape the city life he was leaving behind in Sichuan province. His friends Wu Hua and Yu Jun joined him, and Qiu Han hired a local team to keep the east side locals onboard with his new venture. It worked.

Nanuna was a trendsetter and became the social hub of surfing in southern Hainan. 'Brother Qiu', as Qiu Han was known, became a mentor to all the surfers in the village, and a very close friend. In ten years I witnessed the number of guesthouses on the west side grow from two to 20, while the surf population rose from ten to 100 living in the village full time. But there are barriers to development in Houhai as the surrounding landscape is a military base peppered with rainforest. Houhai was, together with Riyue Wan, soon the hub of Hainan surf life, but both places preserved an unpretentious rugged feel I loved and cherished. And most quality surfs were shared with just a handful of friends.

I was soon part of the blossoming contemporary surf scene in China, working in surf development at many levels and coach of the national and provincial surf teams (with the national team housed in a training centre in Riyue Wan, horizons focused on Olympic success). My colleagues ranged from Wang Yongjian, part of Peter Drouyn's 1985 team and managing director of the Shandong surf team, to Peter Townend, 1976 world champion and head coach of the national surfing team, to Wingnut (who I consider a mentor and a master of style, in and out of the water). Working as a judge at the Qiantang Shootout was a highlight every year as I got to catch up with Mr Wu and Crazy Feng, and thousands of people lined the banks and the bridges to watch, making me somehow relive the sumptuous show of the Song dynasty. The river wave still put my hair on end. Back in the days of the Mid-Autumn festival during the Tang and Song, the wave-riding events took place on the wave depicted by Xia Gui near the Six Harmonies Pagoda. Changes in the river meant that this section became very small, so the Qiantang Shootout ended a few bridges earlier. But it continued to be as spectacular as ever.

Waiting in the judging boat under Bridge Number Nine at dead low tide on the 18th day of the lunar month when the water was running out like a raging creature at 20 knots and the wave appeared as a massive silver line three metres tall was sensational. As it hit the columns under the bridge it produced a beautiful big A-frame, turning from raging white-water to an open face for the first time. Sometimes it barrelled, but no one rode this tube. Nature ruled. And the sound was deafening. A boat failure at that stage would have surely meant tragedy because there were only two safe evacuation points in the whole course, one being the inlet where Mr Wu and the local fishermen docked, the other 36 km upstream, past Crazy Feng, where we finally exited the river.

I spent so much time watching the river wave that I got to know the sections very well. Myself and Matt Wybega, a cameraman who had filmed the bore from a jet ski since 2008, were considered the 'Qiantang bore veterans', and we usually advised the surf crews (who competed in teams of two with the use of jet skis) on the best sections for the respective wind and tide of the day. I also worked as communicator at the event, listening to radio contact between the river authorities, boats and the bore riders, translating between Chinese and English and back, then directing safety instructions to avoid problems. And the potential for problems was massive. Riders had to stay within 100 metres from each bank, while judges and media boats had to stay within a 100 metre range from the leading boat that navigated the safe channels. Riders could not ride under bridges and failing to follow the rules would end up in arrest and immediate suspension from the event. I often intervened on the radio to prevent disasters from happening. These were the rules to play by and safety continued to be the biggest challenge.

An unforgettable Qiantang Shootout was the 2014 one, when our judging boat was positioned right in front of the best right-hand section we called 'pagodas' just past Bridge Number Nine. Here the bore broke on the south side and whelped creating a hypnotic quartet of waves. This was where the highest scores were given during most events. We were close to the bank when I realised that the unbroken first wave had accelerated, and we were caught between the other three waves. I saw the riders up and surfing the first wave as we were about to get hit by the second, third and fourth - all three metres high. I shouted to our captain to speed up as the turbulence was slowing us down massively. We just made it to the deeper channel, with the shoulders of the second and third wave nearly capsizing the boat. Then we overtook the first wave as Hawaiian Jamie O'Brien was carving a clean bottom turn on a huge open face. He arced a sweeping cutback just meters from us as we 'dropped in on him', and, capitalising on the opportunity, audaciously threw a rooster tail of river spray right into the boat.

A Chinese team soon started competing at the Qiantang Shootout, and when together with Peter Townend we selected the first national team in 2014 for the Wanning International Surfing Festival at Riyue Wan, our first team training session was on the river in Hangzhou as CESA's Head of Department (Nana Liu) officially launched the project. This was the beginning of government backing of the national team in light of surfing's inclusion in the 2020 Tokyo Olympics. It was a proud moment, and slowly but surely the new generation of Chinese surfers and event organisers were starting to learn about the *nong chao er*. But despite my experience on the bore, I had still never personally ridden the wave. I resigned to the fact that this was the territory of the *nong chao er* and now China's new generation of surfers. And I was happy about that. But of course I still ride waves on the coast, and that remains my calling.

The monsoon season continues to be the prime time for waves in China as icy northeast winds, born in the cold northern plateau, funnel down the Korean Peninsula, slicing short period swell into the East and South China Sea, making for consistent beachbreak and pointbreak conditions. Summer swells in May to September favour the south facing coasts, and typhoons from August to October can deliver a wide variety of swell directions. These usually form between the Philippines and Guam, near the equator, then gather momentum while moving east and north, achieving maximum strength at around 20° north, then tracking toward the Asian continent, perhaps making landfall in the Philippines, Taiwan, China, Korea or Japan with wind speeds up to 200 mph.

Typhoon swells can be your best friend or your worst enemy in China. Tracking them and surfing their swell is a highlight for all China surfers, or a low-point if you have to evacuate the coastline for a direct hit. It was likely a typhoon swell described in chapter 42 of *Journey to the West* as 'endless lines of waves as far as the eye could see. And all that could be heard was the wind on the waters' as Pig and the Tang Priest were captured by a fire demon called Red Boy. On special swells I continued to see and surf waves likes these, hitting points and reefs and unzipping across bays, held taut by offshores. Usually these went by unridden, and that's why I called China The People's Republic of Empty Waves. And I continued to enjoy every ride.

Of course so much of China's 14,500 km coastline is under regimented use, diligently serving the progress of the nation, be it real estate, tourism development, fish-farms, factories or docks. I've surfed in everything from the sewage coloured browns of Shandong province to the brilliant blues of Guangdong and Hainan, in the ever-present mingling of *yin* and *yang*. Getting to know the locals in the emerging scenes has been exciting. In Fujian there was a small and vibrant surf community from Xiamen, and some stunning unexplored and unridden waves. Further north from Xiamen in Fuzhou has been another surf hub in that province. Close to Shenzhen and Guangzhou on the Dapeng peninsula I found the biggest surf crew outside of Taiwan, Hong Kong and Hainan along one of the most pristine coastlines in the whole country. Then further north the Pinghai area was possibly the most consistent surf area in the Mainland, but also extremely polluted. The Shengsi and Zhoushan archipelagos that I first explored with Callahan in 2007 were beginning to attract surfers from the mainland. And there was a surprisingly old surf community in Qingdao in Shandong, one of the richest provinces in the country, homeland of Confucius and the launch-pad of windsurfing in China.

With such a rich cultural history, it was inevitable that there would be a great revival of interest in Daoism and Buddhism for young Chinese surfers. I couldn't get out of my head what I learned all those years ago from Professor Yang, and became passionate about taking some *Taiji* classes. Surfing so many days of the year, breaks in Beijing were strangely refreshing and culturally interesting. A new girlfriend suggested taking classes with Cheng Xiang, a leading master of the original *Taiji* evolved during the Song dynasty focused on internal meditation with techniques taken from *Qigong*. Cheng Xiang had developed a global reputation, invited by Stanford University to lecture on his ability to apparently control his internal organs (with the same techniques as Professor Yang, who, one day, maybe I'll track down).

After a number of classes with Cheng Xiang I showed him some video clips of the best Chinese female and male longboarders competing at annual world championship events in Riyue Wan. Cheng Xiang was impressed watching Monica Guo, Tie Zhuan and Huang Wei. As Monica Guo took off on the wave, lying prone before standing up, Cheng Xiang said "踏浪而行 *Tà làng ér xíng* (Step on the wave then move)," saying that this was like the beginning of the *Taiji* practice, when he is waiting for the *Qi* to manifest and guide his movements. The *Qi*, or vital energy, is visualised in the shape of a wave, that is coming and will be ridden. He also explained how this was similar to the practice of *Jianqi* which is a sequence of movements used to awaken the sensibility to *Qi*.

The character 踏 *ta* stands for 'step on' in this context and is of course the same word used in my cherished Song and Tang documents for 'treading waves' 踏浪 *ta lang*. I could, again, only fantasise about the different manoeuvres performed by the *nong chao er* when treading waves. In another set of video clips, as Tie Zhuan and Huang Wei walked the board, cross-stepping to the nose, Cheng Xiang said, "巧于用意 *Qiǎoyú yòngyì* (Use your thoughts smartly, with craft appropriately)." He seemed fascinated by the restrained movements, the relationship between body, board and wave, and noted how good surfers limit the movements to what is smart, necessary in that very moment.

Then, as I showed some bigger waves of Chinese shortboarders Qiu Zhuo and Zhu Yan, Cheng Xiang said, "动随 其波静同其得 *Dòngsuí qí bō jìng tóng qí dé* (Move according to this wave, quietly move with it)." He was interested in the way the surfers reacted to the more powerful wave energy, noting how you cannot treat a small wave with the same moves as a big one, because if the energy is low in the wave, you can use *yang* power to cope with it, while huge waves require more *yin*.

As Qiu Zhuo pulled into a serious barrel, filmed at one of the better quality reefbreaks in Hainan, Cheng Xiang said, "动与静和曲身就 *Dòng yǔ jìng hé qǔshēn jiù* (When action and stillness are one, body will move accordingly). 缓阴意随理贯通 *Huǎnyīn yìsuí lǐguàn tōng* (Slow down and the mind will follow)." As the barrelling waves continued Cheng Xiang added, "空而不空 *Kōng ér bù kōng* (Hollow but not empty). 虚而有物 *Xū ér yǒuwù* (Virtual but material)."

This was priceless insight into the deeper meaning and experience of surfing through the lens of Daoism. Cheng Xiang talked about the movements and poses as an explosion of power generated not just by the environment, but also by the personal reaction to it. Similarly, the wave will lead the surfer. If the ancient *nong chao er* thought in such terms, perhaps their wave-riding culture was the perfect marriage of the physical and spiritual. And this is the rich history of China that a new generation of surfers can explore.

China and Chinese language is a huge and scary universe, deep and diverse. But if you take the challenge to learn about it, it can be a marvellous experience. My way into the *mare magnum* of Chinese culture has been through something I know and love, surfing. Getting to assist the birth (or rebirth) of Chinese surf culture, while researching its roots, has been a once in a lifetime opportunity. Chinese surfers train with me in the national team, work with me at surf schools and take me to the hospital when I hit the reef. They are my family out of Italy. They are exploring new waves, forging their own surf lingo and lifestyle, re-connecting with their roots and riding into their future. But Chinese surfing is still small and relatively un-influential. Yet it bisects China, past and present, as sharply as a pintail single fin slices through the almond eye of a tuberide. Will the fabled *nong chao er* be studied for inspiration, used for nationalist pride, or rejected? What is the future of *chong lang* in China? This is now their story as they rediscover the Children of the Tide.

Nicola 'Nik' Zanella
8nicola.zanella8@gmail.com
@nikzanella
@nicola.zanella.735

Printed in April 2019